CROSSROADS
IN
CHRISTIAN GROWTH

W. Loyd Allen

BROADMAN PRESS
Nashville, Tennessee

ISBN: 0-8054-5445-4
Dewey Decimal Classification: 253.5
Subject Heading: PSYCHOLOGY, PASTORAL // COUNSELING
Library of Congress Catalog Card Number: 88-38965
Printed in the United States of America

Unless otherwise indicated Scripture quotations are from the Revised Standard
Version of the Bible, copyrighted 1946, 1952, © 1971, 1973 and are used by permission. Those marked (GNB) are from the *Good News Bible*, the Bible in Today's English Version. Old Testament: Copyright © American Bible Society
1976; New Testament: Copyright © American Bible Society 1966, 1971, 1976.
Used by permission. Those marked (KJV) are from the King James Version of the
Bible.

Library of Congress Cataloging-in-Publication Data

Allen, William Loyd.
    Crossroads in Christian growth / W. Loyd Allen.
      p.   cm. — (The Bible and personal crisis)
    ISBN 0-8054-5445-4
    1. Christian life—1960-   I. Title. II. Series.
BV4501.2.A4344   1989
248.8′4—dc19 .   88-38965

To
Libby
beloved companion on my spiritual journey

Contents

1 Crossroads on the Journey to Christian Maturity 7
2 The Sources of Spiritual Crises 18
3 The View from the Inside 29
4 Crossroads: Traveling Beyond Fairness 58
5 Crossroads: Traveling Beyond Tradition 78
6 Crossroads: Traveling Beyond Personal Understanding .. 103
7 Surrender 128
8 Journey Home Through the Unknown 148

1

Crossroads on the Journey to Christian Maturity

A life without spiritual crises is not authentically Christian. Spiritual crises are a part of healthy faith. Valid Christian faith is known for its ability to overcome difficulties, not for their absence. If your faith is bright and untroubled be forewarned, crises will arise. Where no obstacles to faith appear, faith is nonexistent or stagnant.

What matters is not how many critical crossroads of the spirit are faced nor their degree of difficulty. The crucial point is whether the believer grows in responding to them. Robert Frost's poem, "The Road Not Taken" relates a universal human experience:

> Two roads diverged in a wood, and I—
> I took the one less traveled by,
> And that has made all the difference.[1]

Choices at the crossroads make all the difference. How we respond to the crises in our spiritual lives is the single most important factor in Christian maturity.

This chapter will examine the place of spiritual crises in the life of faith. Our beginning point is: What place do these crises hold in the Christian pilgrimage? Wrestling with the issues which arise from this question will be the subject of the chapters which follow.

Spiritual Crises: Turning Points in a Growth Journey

The Bible presents two key images of Christian life which give a foundation for understanding the place of spiritual crises in our lives. The first image is Christian life as a journey, the second is Christian life as growth. Together these images help us to see our spiritual struggles as stages in a journey of growth toward maturity in Christ.

The Image of Journey

Christians are believers in motion. The image of the Christian life as a journey is neither newfangled nor outdated.[2] The life of faith is a life of journey. The ideal person of faith in the Old Testament is the obedient traveler Abraham, journeying toward a hope unseen (Gen. 12:1; cf. Heb. 11:8). His descendants were the people of God on the Exodus journey, traveling through the wilderness toward the Promised Land. After living in the Promised Land for a time, the depth of their faith was truly measured as they faced another journey, the journey into Exile. Micah 6:8, the individual spiritual life of justice and kindness in one sentence, defines the believer's task as a walk with God.

The New Testament writers continued to recognize the importance of movement in the life of faith. In Matthew 28:19-20 the commissioning of disciples begins with the command, "Go therefore." Some commentators suggest the correct translation is "As you go."[3] If so, the image of Christian disciples as believers on the move is strengthened by the assumption that a command to get them started is not required. Either way disciples are shown as people on pilgrimage.

In the New Testament believers were called followers of "the Way" before they were called "Christians" (compare Acts 9:2 and 11:26). This pointed to a way of life rather than a literal road but does not lessen the impact of the image of disciples as travelers. They were and we are on the way, moving "from faith to faith" (Rom. 1:17, KJV). Christian pilgrims may progress slowly—"The gate is narrow and the way is hard" (Matt. 7:14)—but we are called to "strain forward to what lies ahead" (Phil. 3:13).

The Image of Growth

The second key image or metaphor for Christian life is that of growth. The Christian's journey is growth toward maturity in Christ. The goal of the journey is "mature [personhood]"—full grown-upness—measured against the stature of Christ (Eph. 4:13). Believers are "to grow up in every way into . . . Christ" (v. 15). The parable of the sower as interpreted for disciples in Mark 4:10-20 views fruit-bearing maturity as the desired result of God's activity among His followers. "But those that were sown upon the good soil are the ones who hear the word and accept it and bear fruit, thirtyfold and sixtyfold and a hundredfold" (v. 20). The images of journey and growth together present the Christian as one who is traveling toward maturity in Christ which will yield a miraculous spiritual harvest.

Crossroads on the Growth Journey

The growth journey of believers in Christ is growth in stages. The models of Christian life as growth in the New Testament are pictures drawn from the growth of living things. The growth which occurs on the Christian journey is not the piling up of more of the same—like money growing in a savings account. The seed planted in the good soil does not grow by simply becoming a giant seed. The kingdom of God grows from tiny blade to stalk to fruit-bearing maturity (Mark 4:22-29). The growth in Christ is like the growth of the human body (Eph. 4:15-16). This growth in stages toward maturity is the way a living faith develops.

The spiritual life as journey also reflects this truth of stages. From the final destination looking back, faith's pilgrimage may seem like one continuous unbroken path; but, for those of us still on the way, it appears as a series of crossroads where decisions must be made about which way to take. Persons arriving at a new destination can look back on their trip as a single route, but this route is made up of stages separated by turning points or crossroads. The trav-

eler on the way scans the street signs, counts the traffic
lights, checks the handwritten directions, trying to decide
which turn to take at each important crossroad. Each stage
of Christian growth requires the one growing to face a
choice, a crossroad decision. The turning points between
the stages in the faith journey are spiritual crises.

When these crossroads are absent there is no journey;
where there is no journey there is no growth; and without
growth there is no Christian faith. Life on the journey to
Christian maturity is life familiar with crossroads.

Christ at the Crossroads

Jesus Christ is central to Christian life as journey and as
growth. Following Jesus is the beginning of our Christian
growth journey. Mark's Gospel reveals this with powerful
simplicity. Jesus called, the fishermen left their boats, and
followed; Jesus called, Levi left his tax table, and followed
(Mark 1:16-20; 2:14). Jesus calls, we follow, the journey
starts. Jesus is the Way which we follow (John 14:6). As the
call to follow suggests, we go where He leads us; and He
leads us toward Himself. The goal we travel toward is Jesus
(Phil. 3:14). Jesus Christ is the beginning, the middle, and
the end of our journey toward grown-upness as children of
God. Christians move from faith to faith through the crossroads of spiritual growth in Christ.

Spiritual Crises: Crossroads or Detours?

Every personal crisis, however, is not a crossroad in faith.
Not every time of difficulty is a challenge to a new stage in
Christian growth. Some obstacles are faced and overcome
without much change in the shape or direction of faith. I
call these crises detours rather than actual crossroads.

Detours

Personal crises of great significance—family, health, or
job crises—are the common lot of humanity. Each of these

turning points is decided by persons according to the measure of their faith. Each is faith related, but not every one
necessarily calls for a redirected faith.

Some personal crises may be resolved by calling upon resources within one's present relationship to God. Others call
us to form new ways of understanding and relating to God
which were previously unimagined. Crises of the first type
are not truly crossroads but rather detours which call upon
the traveler to go around an obstacle in order to move on.
The direction of life and the way of relating to God after
detours are much the same as before the crisis.

Crossroads

Spiritual crises, on the other hand, call for a deeper, more
radical redirection. In the faith to faith journey, faith
changes and so do the faithful. These changes often occur
along with other personal crises but the outcome of spiritual
crisis is more thoroughly transforming.

The nature of faith demands this. Faith determines the
meaning and shape of life. Faith is not one branch among
many on the tree of life, it is that which gives shape and
identity to the whole. The transformation in a stage from
faith to faith is as thorough as the transformation from seed
to sapling.

The way chosen in a spiritual crisis is a change that
changes everything, a piece that alters the whole. The old
way of believer and God relating is reformed, it is redirected. In journey terms, it is as if the traveler took a detour
that never returned to the old road but proceeded toward
life's destination by a new route.

A question asked in the Book of Psalms shows this difference between detours and crossroads in faith. The setting
for the question is the Exile. Ripped out of their homeland
in the sixth century BC by the Babylonian conquest, God's
grieving chosen people wept on a foreign riverbank. Their
enemies taunted them, saying: "Sing us one of the songs of

Zion!" (Ps. 137:3). The psalmist, in personal crisis created by this national calamity, asked: "How shall we sing the Lord's song in a foreign land?" (v. 4).

The psalmist had long found help in the songs of the Lord, identified by him with the land of Zion. But this new crisis called for something beyond the old ways of relating to God. How could the songs of Zion be sung in the land of those who had conquered Zion? God had been understood as Zion's God, yet Zion was far away. Could the God of the land of Zion be praised in the land of a victorious enemy far away? Never again could the writer view himself, Israel, or God in the same light as before the conquest.

The psalm ends in bitterness, blessing those who kill the babies of the Babylonians (v. 9). A new way of relating to God was required to redirect the journey in faith being taken by the psalmist with his God. The writer was at a crossroad. The direction taken at this turning point was an affirmation of Israel's God as God beyond national borders, and this redirected faith for the people of Abraham's God forever.

The same journey.—In applying this Exile event to our faith, I am not saying that Christian growth means moving from Christian faith to faith of some other kind, or that faith on the first part of the journey is less than Christian. Some things are constant. Always the Christian is the same traveler, always the guide is the same unchanging Spirit, always the grace of God is the unfailing source of strength for the journey. These are certainties Christians can count on whether in crisis or out, truths from which we can draw assurance as faith's expression changes on the way to maturity.

Redirected.—On the other hand, God's call to change during life's journey is just as certain as His steadfastness within that journey. Striving toward the goal set before us is not just a matter of accumulated distance. A believer is not a jogger on a circular track covering the same old ground again and again, adding up the miles. We are not just moving, we are moving toward a goal. The way to that goal may lead through unfamiliar territory.

The life of faith is like a long trip covering many different types of territory—trackless sea and desert as well as smooth highway, level forest path along with steep mountain trail. The same traveler at one stage in the journey might need to be a sailor, at another a camel driver on caravan, at still another a lonely hiker on a solitary trek or a rock climber on a sheer granite face. The same traveler is both the sailor and the camel rider, the hiker and the rock climber. The journey is one, there is but one traveler, but they both change along the way. The one who arrives at the final destination is the one who began the journey yet is changed because of directions taken at certain crossroads along the way.

Spiritual Crises: Crossroads or Roadblocks?

As we have seen, crossroads appear in the lives of all Christians which cause us to wonder which direction to turn, which path to take in following Jesus. Temporarily stymied in our growth as believers, frustrated at the lack of ground gained, we sometimes feel roadblocked in faith until a choice can be made. To grow in faith we must turn these roadblocks into crossroads, these obstacles into turning points toward further Christlikeness.

The Importance of Choice

Some spiritual crises become crossroads where the road taken leads the traveler toward Christian maturity. Others roadblock Christian growth leaving a stunted, immature Christian. The difference lies in the choices made. We can examine spiritual crises in our Christian journey in order to learn from them how to decide for Christ in crisis. Like an athletics coach stopping a game film to explain a crucial play, important stages in Christian development can be pulled out from the flow of life's events and studied to increase our ability to follow the Holy Spirit's leadership.

Crises and choice cannot be separated. The Latin root of *crisis* means "to part" or "to separate." A crisis is a turning point, a parting of the ways. At the end of a spiritual crisis, a choice of direction will have been made, things will have gone one way or the other.

The choices in crises are difficult to make. During crisis a blend of fear and hope persists. The Chinese sign for crisis points to this. It is a combination of the figures for "danger" and "opportunity."[4] New directions emerge from emergencies. Once the traveler is back on the right track the pilgrimage of faith proceeds, but much of importance to Christian discipleship and growth lies in the past choice at the last crossroad and waits ahead at the next.

The Traveler as Chooser

In genuine spiritual crises we find that the usual ways of understanding ourselves under God prove unable to keep us going on our journey as Christians. Such roadblocks require us to take a new direction. If we have spent all our lives on a well-marked roadway and then cast by events or led by inner calling to the edge of a trackless desert we will fear becoming lost. At the juncture of the old way and the new way the traveler becomes chooser, and the choice is a choice of faith.

For the Christian, choosing is not strictly a matter of individual choice, of making our best guess. It is a matter of turning over the control center of our lives to the Holy Spirit so that our choice is in line with God's will. Crossroads with strange and unfamiliar directives from God are spiritual crises in which God is calling us to leave the land of the familiar and to move on to the unseen Promised Land. Like the psalmist in Babylon we are called to envision God in a new and larger way. These are moments of anxiety and expectation when one's relationship to God, self, and others hangs in the balance. Saying "Choose God" is easy but doing so in unfamiliar circumstances is not.

Choosing Rightly: Orienteering and Discernment

To choose God in spiritual crisis the believer must become reoriented. To orient oneself means to turn in the right direction. The noun *orient* originally meant the direction of the rising sun. Travelers halted by darkness could orient themselves by turning toward the east as the sun rose. Like the psalmist by the riverbank, anyone of us may be spiritually disoriented. We may not know how to turn to the God of Zion in a strange land. Only a redirecting of our faith in Yahweh can put us back on the path of faith.

Christian travelers in spiritual crisis must pause to reorient themselves by turning toward the risen Son. At baptism early Christians symbolized commitment to the Christian way by first facing west (the direction of darkness, where the sun goes down) and renouncing Satan; then they turned toward the east (the direction of sunrise) and owned Christ.[5] Throughout life Christians repeat this turning to Christ for direction in the journey of faith.

Some learning is involved in become reoriented. At our college we teach a survival skill called orienteering. It is the art of finding one's way through an unknown area by using a map and compass. A compass is used to determine a direction of travel when familiar landmarks are lacking or when the "orienteer" wishes to be absolutely certain of the correct course of action.

Orienteering in the spiritual life is called discernment. Discernment is the activity which has helped Christian pilgrims determine their direction of travel through the centuries. To discern means to separate one thing from another, the right way from the wrong way. In 1 Corinthians 12:10

Paul named spiritual discernment (*diakriseis pneumatōn* in the Greek) as a gift of the Holy Spirit. *The Westminster Dictionary of Christian Spirituality* defines this gift of discernment as the skill to know the "orientation or direction according to the gospel principle"[6] of the inner spirits urging a person toward one choice or another.

To follow God through spiritual crises is to seek to know the Spirit which consistently points us toward the Son of God who is our final goal. Following the direction of the Spirit, even when God redirects our path, is the way of Christian life.

This activity of choosing to follow the Spirit is intensely important at certain times in our lives. These times are spiritual crises when the ways of making progress which had before allowed us to move toward our goal may have to be surrendered to new means. The Christian's continuing progress hinges on the ability to follow the Spirit's leading in the right direction. This choosing is the Christian act of discernment. The rest of this book is intended to strengthen the believer's understanding of the crossroads in Christian growth so that discernment may be increased and the Way made plainer.

Conclusions

In summary, spiritual crises are a normal part of the journey to maturity in Christ. These crises are turning points between the stages of faith's development. Though all personal crises have a faith factor in them they are not all spiritual crises. True spiritual crises are changes that alter the whole of life. For such crises to become crossroads in the journey and not roadblocks to faith, the traveler must become chooser. Choice is the key to spiritual growth. Spiritual crises lead to spiritual growth as believers orient themselves toward Christ. The practice of turning toward Christ in spiritual crises is made possible through the Spirit's gift of discernment.

Notes

1. From *The Poetry of Robert Frost*, Edward Connery Lathem, ed. (New York: Copyright © 1916, 1923, 1928, 1930, 1943, 1945, 1947, 1949, © 1967 by Holt, Rinehart and Winston, Inc.), p. 105. Used by permission of Henry Holt and Company, Inc.

2. The most popular book ever written in English, John Bunyan's *The Pilgrim's Progress*, 1676, is a classic allegory of the spiritual life as journey. Recently numerous authors writing of the spiritual life from a more psychologically oriented stance have also adopted the journey motif. See Scott Peck's bestseller, *The Road Less Travelled* (New York: Simon and Schuster, 1978) or Benedict J. Groeschel's *Spiritual Passages: The Psychology of Spiritual Development* (New York: Crossroad, 1984).

3. See Frank Stagg, "Matthew," *The Broadman Bible Commentary*, Vol. 8 (Nashville: Broadman Press, 1969), p. 252.

4. Howard Clinebell, *Basic Types of Pastoral Care and Counseling*, revised and enlarged edition (Nashville: Abingdon Press, 1984), p. 209.

5. Josef A. Jungmann, *The Early Liturgy* (Notre Dame, Ind.: University of Notre Dame Press, 1959), p. 82.

6. Ernest E. Larkin, "Discernment of Spirits," *The Westminster Dictionary of Christian Spirituality*, ed. Gordon S. Wakefield (Philadelphia: The Westminster Press, 1983), p. 115.

2

The Sources
of Spiritual Crises

Persons at spiritual turning points are looking for direction. Asking, "How did I come to this turning point?" helps answer, "Where do I go from here?" If believers can discern the source behind the present conflict, they can better chart a future course.

This chapter will seek the sources of spiritual crisis. Do they rise from within us or are they forced upon us from without? Do these crises come from God or Satan? Spiritual crossroads in Jesus' life will guide this exploration for the sources of spiritual crisis. At different stages in His life He faced spiritual crises like ours yet stayed perfectly on track toward God. After reviewing the main sources of spiritual crossroads we will look for them in Jesus' experience, closing this chapter with some insights drawn from His example.

Developmental or Conditional

Spiritual crossroads can be divided by source into two kinds: developmental and conditional. Developmental crises are those which unfold naturally in a familiar pattern. They are a normal and generally predictable part of spiritual growth.[1] Conditional crises are those which arise from surrounding conditions. They have their main source in the individual believer's circumstances. These sources show more variety from believer to believer than do developmental sources. Often they are unexpected, unpredictable, and appear suddenly.[2] Their source is not routine, not to be expected on the usual route.

Developmental Spiritual Crises

A natural unfolding is at the root of the developmental sources. A rosebud develops by slowly unfolding its petals into the full expression of a mature flower. The pattern of this unfolding is natural, orderly, and fairly predictable.

Human growth is somewhat the same. Demonstration of this in physical growth is unnecessary; however, it is also true of inner growth.[3] My daughter is five weeks old. She has just begun to develop the ability to smile. Recently a friend leaned over and greeted her as she lay in my arms. Previously the response to his greetings had been an emotionless gaze from a rather expressionless face, but this time our friend was rewarded with a toothless grin. "There's really somebody in there!" he exclaimed. "That's it, Baby Girl, let yourself out." This unfolding of the person within the person is like the unfolding of a rosebud. It occurs according to the laws or patterns of natural growth.

The unfolding or development of spiritual maturity is like the unfolding of human personality. It occurs by God's design according to the pattern of human growth. Some spiritual crises arise naturally as this growth occurs.

In this way growth brings spiritual crisis. Right now my daughter's choices are made mostly by her parents, but her growth will change that. It will soon allow her to make more and more choices for herself. She will come to a crossroad where she must choose between continuing to rely on her parents' faith or making a personal commitment of her own. If she becomes a Christian she will need to choose the kind of work best suited for an expression of her Christian calling. She will need to discern if her calling is to marriage or remaining single.

All through life such crossroads will occur naturally as she faces choices about children of her own; the disappointment of finding out that some personal goals are unreachable; and the reality of the final crisis, her own death. Each of these crises is a likely setting for spiritual crossroads. Each will occur ordinarily as a part of the human journey toward maturity. They are predictable because growth brings crises.

Conditional Spiritual Crises

In the growth of living things, some built-in crossroads are a usual part of the process of growth. The bud must bloom to become fruitful. These are critical turning points, but they are not the only source of crisis. Outside conditions also affect the growth journey of living things. If a drought occurs at the time for blooming, the plant may never turn toward fruitfulness.

Faith is a living thing. Outside circumstances can influence its journey to mature expression. Conditional sources of spiritual crises are like the drought: they come from the outside, unpredictably. By conditional spiritual crises, I mean those crises which arise from the circumstances around us. They often catch us unawares. Their source is more from the outside than from the inside. The untimely death of a loved one; the cherished dream destroyed by circumstances beyond our control; the turmoil created by natural disasters such as tornadoes or unnatural disasters such as war[4] are sources of conditional spiritual crises.

Conditional spiritual crises may be common, but they are not natural. They are not crises which every person can expect to experience if he or she lives long enough. For instance, not everyone experiences divorce or bankruptcy. These may be familiar human experiences; but they are rooted in circumstance, not growth.

Development and Conditions Combined

If you have been thinking of your own personal spiritual crises and have been trying to decide whether they are developmental or conditional, you may find yourself a bit confused. As you and I think of the spiritual crossroads we have gone through in our lives, the line between developmental and conditional crises seems to fade. This is normal.

In life's experiences, spiritual crises are hybrids shaped from developmental and conditional materials. A hybrid is something with more than one source. Crossroads in spiritual growth arise both from the maturity of the travelers and the circumstances surrounding them. The balance of inward or outward concerns may vary. Labeling a crises as one or the other is a matter of deciding the main influence. In changes of faith's direction, both sources are usually involved to some degree. The example of Jesus yields a deeper understanding of this connection.

Crossroads in Jesus' Life

We walk a path Jesus has already trod. He walked through the crossroads of Christian growth. Luke 2:52 says He grew in wisdom and stature. Jesus experienced spiritual crisis because He grew and growth brings crisis. Jesus was "one who in every respect has been tempted as we are" (Heb. 4:15). Hebrews 5:8 says He "learned" and "[was] made perfect" (v. 9) through the unfolding of His own human experience. These crossroads prepared Him for the final great crisis of the cross.

His supreme example for us lies not in His avoidance of spiritual crises but in His unerring ability to stay oriented toward God. The crises He faced came from developmental and conditional sources. The Scriptures illustrate these in Jesus' life. From them we can find aid for our own spiritual journey.

The Crossroad of Personal Responsibility

Jesus' trip to Jerusalem in Luke 2:41-52 is a good example of a developmental spiritual crisis.[5] Jesus, at twelve years of age, went with Mary and Joseph to Jerusalem. As His parents journeyed back home to Nazareth, they realized He was not with them. Returning to Jerusalem they found Him after three days search. He was in the Temple talking with the religious authorities. Mary, the anxious mother, scolded her boy for His apparent disregard of their feelings. Jesus thought they should understand He would be in His Heavenly Father's house. They did not. In obedience to them He returned to Nazareth.

The child Jesus was growing up. His unfolding faith caused Him to reach out and explore the facts of faith for Himself. This independence caused anxiety to His parents. The questions at this crossroad are common to all children at the turning point between childhood and adulthood: What was His responsibility in obedience to God? How could Jesus fulfill this responsibility without some independence from Mary and Joseph; yet if He exercised this freedom, how could He honor father and mother? His childhood faith was unfolding, developing into more mature and accountable faith.

The developmental spiritual crisis faced by children beginning to think for themselves is not the central point of this story—Jesus' true Sonship is—but the main message is made clear through a crisis common to growing up. Jesus' journey toward maturity made its way through the common crossroads of human growth.[6] All of the normal crises arising from human growth may be occasions for us to learn the will of God. As we shall see, the conditional spiritual crises are also ways to "[learn] obedience" (Heb. 5:8).

The Crossroad of True Calling

Jesus' temptations in the wilderness show Him wrestling with the spiritual crisis of His calling (Mark 1:12-13; Matt. 4:1-11; Luke 4:1-13). This was a developmental crisis with choices shaped by conditional sources.

As a young adult, Jesus was about to start His public ministry. Just after being proclaimed the Son of God at baptism,

Jesus was driven by the Spirit into the wilderness. There He was tempted by the devil to be false to this calling. Jesus, like others on the journey of human growth who are wrestling with choices about the exact shape of their vocation, was experiencing a developmental crisis. Earlier in Jesus' life, at age twelve in the Temple, for instance, a crisis the shape of this one would have been premature. Later in Jesus' life these questions would already be answered. They unfolded at the ordinary and correct time in His human pilgrimage.

The form of the temptations, however, is conditional. Mark's version sets Jesus' temptations in the middle of a great struggle between the forces of good and evil, but it does not give a blow-by-blow description. Matthew and Luke do. Jesus was tempted to prove His Sonship in three dead-end ways. Each of the three would have been a roadblock on His spiritual journey.

In Matthew's telling, Jesus was first tempted to prove His Sonship by making bread from stones. Some Jews of His day demanded just such a miracle as proof of messiahship (John 6:30 f.). Next He was tempted to perform the miraculous stunt of surviving a leap from the Temple. He could test God's affirmation and, at the same time, draw a large following from those who demanded signs. Finally Jesus was tempted to choose political power to establish Himself. That the Messiah would lead the nation Israel to replace Rome as the center of a worldy empire was taken for granted by those awaiting the Messiah in Jesus' day, including His own disciples (see John 6:15 and Acts 1:6). Jesus rejected all of these choices. Discerning a better way He turned in a new direction.

These temptations show that Jesus' stage in life and the expectations of the people of His day combined to present Him with a spiritual crisis. The stage in life was the developmental source, the circumstances of Jewish expectations the conditional. The way these two combined to form a crossroad in Jesus' spiritual journey is captured by Frank Stagg's final statement on the Matthean temptations: "Jesus on the threshold of his ministry was compelled to choose the road he would travel, against impulse and against popular expectation but in obedience to the will of God."[7] This is the description of a turn made at a crossroad in spiritual growth.

The Crossroad of the Crucifixion

The road from the temptations led to Golgotha. The cross was at the center of Jesus' last and greatest spiritual crisis. No analysis can plumb the depths of God's act at Calvary, but no other source reveals so rich an understanding of our personal spiritual crises. To place what we know about our own spiritual crises alongside the supreme crisis of the cross is to come near to the heart of the Christian journey.

In the next chapter we will seek the shape of spiritual crises by closely examining the cross of Christ. For now let us simply note that the Book of Hebrews' commentary on this spiritual crisis in Jesus' life speaks of Jesus being tested and tempted in all ways as we are and that the cross is the supreme example of his response to these spiritual crises. It was a time of suffering, learning, and perfecting (Heb. 2:10; 5:7-10).

Crossroads in Our Lives

What can we learn by looking at the sources of spiritual crises in the experience of Jesus? Three things: first, spiritual crossroads are not evil; second, spiritual crossroads are dangerous; and third, no one is excused from the lessons of spiritual crisis.

Crossroads Are Not Evil

First, spiritual crossroads are not sinful. If you are suffering, questioning, confused as to where you should turn next in faith, these are not sure signs that you have sinned. Jesus suffered as you are suffering; He did not sin (Heb. 2:10).

God is the source of developmental spiritual crises. He has built into the life cycle of those created in His image developmental turning points which require faithful choices. Such crossroads on the way to spiritual maturity are a part of God's good creation and are therefore good themselves. Jesus experienced these as He matured and so will we as we journey onward in faith. Remember, it was the Spirit which drove Jesus into the wilderness where He was tempted.

Conditional spiritual crises are somewhat more complex. The conditions which surround us are sometimes shaped by sinful actions but they are still not evidence that a particular spiritual crisis is evil. Though the Spirit drove Jesus into the wilderness, the temptations He faced there were formed from popular expectations of the promised Messiah. That Jesus was tempted by these traditional but mistaken interpretations is no sign that Jesus was in sin.

Remember the disciples' question and Jesus' answer in John 9:1-4. Upon meeting a blind man, they asked, "Rabbi, who sinned, this man or his parents, that he was born blind?" Jesus answered, "It was not that this man sinned, or his parents, but that the works of God might be made manifest in him." The conditional sources of our personal spiritual crises are like that. They are not a sign of our sin, but an opportunity for spiritual growth. Persons in spiritual crisis need not take their situation as a sign of their poor standing with God.

Crossroads Are Dangerous

I have not forgotten Satan. The place of evil in spiritual crossroads is the second lesson to be learned from studying their sources. While the questions and confusion of being at a crossroad are not bad in themselves, Satan uses such events as an opportunity to give us wrong directions. Spiritual crossroads are times of great danger.

Reflect on Jesus as He was led into the wilderness by the Spirit. He was met by the devil who tried to misdirect the developmental crisis of Jesus' vocational calling. Providing bread, performing miracles, presiding over all kingdoms— each was a legitimate part of Jesus' calling, but not in the manner the devil presented them. As we make choices at spiritual crossroads, we must be careful to obey the Word of God and not the rewording of Satan.

God-given circumstances which are sent to test our faith may become devilish temptations by evil distortion. In the original language of the New Testament both testing and temptation are based on the word *peirazō*. Testing is motivated by the desire to increase faith, temptation by the desire to encourage sin. Both are trials, the first is from God and the second from Satan. A study of the sources of spiritual crises reveals that each is present within spiritual crossroads.

Learning From Spiritual Crossroads

Third, no one is exempt from the lessons to be learned in spiritual crisis. Even Jesus had to face the dangers of the tests and temptations of spiritual crossroads. He learned obedience through them; He matured through suffering their dangers.

At His crossroads Jesus learned to listen to the direction of God. He had always desired to obey God's direction; He had always had an ear for God's guidance. These were necessary for His spiritual maturity but they were not enough. Standing at the crossroads He had to act on these commitments as God called His Child forward from familiar security to untraveled territory. Obedience to this call required Jesus to hear the voice of God above the misdirections of the Evil One. This was Jesus' act of discernment.

This experience was necessary for the spiritual growth of Jesus. Through such crises Hebrews 5:8-9 says He "learned obedience" and was "made perfect." To obey originally meant to hear. Jesus learned to hear God at the crossroads where different voices called out conflicting directions. By following the voice He learned to hear in these trials He became perfect, unfolding into full maturity.

Jesus' response to the sources of spiritual crisis teaches us that there are no shortcuts to Christian maturity. Every child of God must learn the lesson of obedience at the crossroads where anxiety and danger are part of the journey. Do not be surprised to meet them. Be prepared to pass through them by discerning the voice of your Guide.

Jesus' example can teach us that accepting the tough decisions which developmental spiritual crises bring us is a part of life's gift to us. His example can teach us that we must discern the rightful use of the circumstances in which we find ourselves. Finally, His example can show us that there is no other way to maturity except by traveling through spiritual crossroads. Only at the crossroads in Christian growth can we learn to listen, discern, and obey.

In the next chapter we will investigate the shape of spiritual crises from within. We will seek to learn how to hear and obey the guidance of the Holy Spirit at spiritual crossroads.

Notes

1. In describing developmental spiritual crises I do not imply by words such as "natural" or "predictable" a lesser degree of intensity or importance. Many developmental crises such as birth and death are of the utmost importance and spiritual intensity.

2. Conditional crises are sometimes called *accidental* or *situational* because of the environmental source of the stress. See Howard Clinebell, *Basic Types of Pastoral Care and Counseling*, revised and enlarged edition (Nashville: Abingdon Press, 1984), pp. 186-87, and David K. Switzer, *The Minister as Crisis Counselor* (Nashville: Abingdon Press, 1974), pp. 44-45.

3. The growth of human personality and spirit is different in that the rosebud has no choice in development but people do by virtue of the image of God within them. This unique aspect of human spiritual development will be addressed more fully later.

4. The psalmist of chapter 1 was suffering a spiritual crisis which had its source in war.

5. The main message of Luke 2:41-52 is that Jesus is the Son of God, but the setting for this affirmation is a crisis of human spiritual development.

6. See James W. Fowler, *Stages of Faith* (San Francisco: Harper and Row, 1981), for a study of some of the major points of contact between human development and faith development.

7. Frank Stagg, "Matthew," *The Broadman Bible Commentary*, Vol. 8 (Nashville: Broadman Press, 1969), p. 99.

3

The View from the Inside

Like a mountaintop observer looking down on a winding valley road, chapter 1 presented spiritual crossroads from a distance, giving their setting within life's whole spiritual journey. In chapter 2 we asked why these turning points arise and what their sources have to tell us as we travel on life's way. Now we are ready to move off the mountain and look at the shape of spiritual crises up close. In this chapter we will enter spiritual crossroads, look at them from the inside, and seek a way out. An inside view of spiritual crossroads will help us pilgrims recognize landmarks in our personal experiences which may help us find our way home someday.

Some structural details are common to all spiritual crises. As Christian growth proceeds, each spiritual crossroad is entered, endured, and exited.[1] Each of these three parts of crises has its own characteristics. Underlying all of them is one universal form—the cross of Jesus Christ. Spiritual crises are cross shaped. Jesus' anticipation, suffering, and transformation on the way of the cross is the Christian pattern for shaping our own spiritual crossroads.

His cross is a model and more, it is an ever-present source of power and new life. Day by day we are called to mold our lives to the shape of the cross. Jesus told His disciples to take up their cross daily and follow Him (Luke 9:23). Spiritual crossroads are the crucial moments in this following and we do well to remember that the word *crucial* has its source in the crucifixion of Christ.

Entryway

Spiritual crossroads are entered through life's difficulties. A problem or need appears in the life of the believer. Life's ordinary path changes and the traveler enters territory which is unfamiliar and hard.

The surest sign that a genuine spiritual crises is being entered is the failure of tried and true methods to solve the problem. If a way through the difficulty is found without much trouble and the believer continues on in life with business as usual, no spiritual crisis has occurred. It is as if a person rafting on a calm river encountered rapids but slid quickly and easily through them to calm water on the other side. If the problem is an entry into spiritual crisis, however, the rapids are not soon over. Instead the channel becomes narrower and narrower, the bluffs of the now raging river become steeper and steeper. Nothing the rafter does seems to help and, in a rushing foamy roar, the traveler is pulled helplessly towards the jagged edges of disaster, searching frantically for a way out.

The Three Steps

Three steps take one into spiritual crisis: first, normal efforts which fail; then intensified effort which also fails; and third a grasping at ways which are farther and farther out on the edge of helpful behavior. Spiritual crossroads are entered through problems which do not yield to the usual coping methods. If the standard means of finding a way out of difficulty fail, we usually intensify our efforts. We try harder, doing the same things with more energy. If this proves unsuccessful, anxiety increases, we look into our past experience for other tools, for old tricks seldom used. As these fall short we apply means which are designed less well to fit the situation.

Imagine a hostage in an isolated area who has taken a

ring of keys from a sleeping guard and now sits in the kid-napper's car feverishly trying key after key in the ignition. If the most likely looking ones fail, the fumbling hostage tries keys less and less probable in size and appearance. Tension rises, desperation looms. As the last key fails we are not surprised to see the prisoner hopelessly pounding the steering column in frustration.

Like hostages trying to get moving again, persons in the entryway of spiritual crossroads run through their choices and resources without success. They are unable to get away from their problems. Often they turn to the most improbable of spiritual resources. Perhaps childish bargaining or other long-abandoned faith expressions rise again. In the most extreme cases mental illness may result as despair or ritual compulsion takes over. The Christian at crossroad becomes, like John Bunyan's Pilgrim, mired in the Slough of Despond, unable to find the path out; trapped in Doubting Castle which is ruled by the giant, Despair.[2] The person has seen the entryway to a crossroad in faith.

This entry into a crisis in Christian growth may occur suddenly or gradually. Spiritual terrain can change quickly or slowly. River rafters may suddenly hear the roar of a deep falls ahead and drop quickly into dangerous white water, or they may gradually drift into swifter and swifter currents, realizing too late that they are in the grip of dangerous rapids. Mountain hikers may abruptly come to the edge of a cliff or they may slog slowly along as their surroundings change from lush forest to barren rocks. They may realize unexpectedly that their easy path has vanished.

A Historical Example

The great Protestant Reformer Martin Luther presents us with a classic example of entry into spiritual crisis. Luther, a German Christian of the sixteenth century, was road-blocked in his spiritual journey by a sense of his own sinfulness. He sought his way out of this guilt by following the directions of the church of his time.[3]

First he became a monk, living the holy life of a priest to please God. When this did not remove the obstacle of his guilt he intensified his monkery. Luther biographer Roland Bainton quoted Luther as saying:

> I was a good monk, and I kept the rule of my order so strictly that I may say that if ever a monk got to heaven by his monkery it was I. All my brothers in the monastery who knew me will bear me out. If I had kept on any longer, I should have killed myself with vigils, prayers, reading, and other work.[4]

This self-help did not work, so Luther sought salvation by transfer. He made a pilgrimage to Rome seeking indulgences from the storehouse of merits in that holy city. He hoped to transfer some of their excess goodness into his own depleted account by acts of penance. They were not adequate to the task.

During these trials Luther was moving toward an enormous spiritual crossroad. He tried one proven solution after another, but to no avail. He intensified his efforts; he tried extraordinary means. However successful such measures may have been for others, for Luther they were powerless to remove what he called his *Anfechtung*. This German word means a test sent by God or a temptation of the devil.[5] Failing to find one English word equal to *Anfechtung* Bainton wrote: "It is all the doubt, turmoil, pang, tremor, panic, despair, desolation, and desperation which invade the spirit of man."[6] In Luther we can recognize the interior view of an entry into spiritual crisis.

The Example of Paul

Luther's deliverance began with Bible reading. In the Bible Luther met one who seemed to have been through what he himself was experiencing, one who had worked as hard as Luther to hack out his own spiritual path. This man, Paul, described himself as "advanced in Judaism beyond many of my own age among my people, so extremely zealous was I for the traditions of my fathers" (Gal. 1:14). He was "circumcised on the eighth day, of the people of Israel, of the tribe of Benjamin, a Hebrew born of Hebrews; as to the law a Pharisee, as to zeal a persecutor of the church, as to righteousness under the law blameless" (Phil. 3:5-6).

Luther met in Scripture one who in his desire to move onward in his spiritual growth had gone to the limit in zeal. Paul had stood holding the coats of the crowd who stoned Stephen, consenting to his death (Acts 7:58; 8:1). Here was one who knew the desperation of spiritual crisis, who had stood at a major spiritual crossroad. In The Letter of Paul to the Romans, Luther read:

> I can will what is right, but I cannot do it. For I do not do the good I want, but the evil I do not want is what I do. Wretched man that I am! Who will deliver me from this body of death? (Rom. 7:19,24).

This is the cry of one well acquainted with the entranceway of spiritual crossroads.

The Example of Jesus

Jesus, of course, was the answer to Luther's quest and Paul's question; but, before we oversimplify things, let us look at the entry to crisis Jesus faced. The Gospels reveal Jesus marching relentlessly toward Jerusalem and the cross throughout His ministry. Because we know this and because we know the happy ending we often fail to see clearly the entryway into the spiritual crisis of the cross.

Early in His ministry Jesus rejected the traditional means to leadership among His people: bread, miracles, and political power.[7] This narrowing of options finally led to the agonizing scene in the Garden of Gethsemane. There, greatly distressed and troubled, describing Himself as "sorrowful, even unto death," Jesus prayed for a detour: "He fell on the ground and prayed that, if it were possible, the hour might pass from him" (Mark 14:32-36). Jesus' prayer for deliverance is not the whole revelation of the way of the cross, but the way to His cross was through the Garden. So goes the way to ours, His followers.

Conclusion

This is the form of the entry to a spiritual crossroad: difficulties which seem unbearable and unsolvable, problems which do not respond to ordinary or extraordinary efforts to remove them. Only the foolish would ignore the possibility of catastrophe in these circumstances, but that is not the only possibility. This slippery grip on the brink of despair has been shared by others who have been lifted onward to higher things. Remember Jesus, remember Paul, remember Luther. From them to us comes the insight that this thin ledge of desperation is potentially the approach to Christian growth and progress.

Inside

Before that potential can become reality, though, the crisis must be endured. Inside a spiritual crossroad the sense of loss and disorientation outweighs any sense of happy expectation. Having entered a spiritual crossroads the traveler stands at a disturbing turning point. This is a time of decision, full of opportunity and danger. It is a stage of endurance, for here suffering is inevitable and often intense. It is under such conditions that Christians may grow in likeness to Jesus. He is the trailblazer made perfect through suffering; we are to follow His path (Heb. 2:10).

Three options are open to the believers standing in the center of a spiritual crisis. They can remain where they are,

they can turn around and go back, or they can go forward.[8]
Two of these choices are dead ends and the third is full of
danger.

Standing Still

One choice for travelers at crossroads is to try to remain
where they are, neither going backward nor forward. To
stay put in spiritual crisis is destructive to spiritual life. Surrounded by questions and confusion some seem to believe it
is better to live with present circumstances than to risk the
unknown. This is sheer unbelief, the opposite of faith which
is "the assurance of things hoped for, the conviction of things
not seen" (Heb. 11:1).

Paul, imprisoned at Caesarea, spoke to the governor Felix
"about justice and self-control and future judgment" (Acts
24:25). Felix became alarmed and told Paul to go away for
awhile, that he would call for him later. Off and on for two
years Felix discussed faith with Paul. Apparently Felix was
often able to put off his alarm enough to avoid a decision.
He remained at the crossroad.

An old gospel hymn tells of a train which is bound for
glory. I picture Felix and those like him standing on a platform where several tracks cross, unable to decide which
train goes home. Though choosing a train has an element of
risk, to stand forever on the platform is to miss the trip altogether. One might as well turn back and unpack.

Turning Back

Turning back is a second possibility for the travelers at
crossroads. The Bible is clear about the consequences of
turning back: "If he shrinks back, my soul has no pleasure
in him" (Heb. 10:38). Jesus said: "No one who puts his hand
to the plow and looks back is fit for the kingdom of God"
(Luke 9:62). Reflection upon the nature of the Christian life
easily reveals the basis of such a hard judgment. Christian

faith is a living, growing faith, a life in motion. To turn back
is to stop growing; to stop growing is to die. Christians in
spiritual crisis can no more turn back and live than a rose in
bloom can return to its bud. Faith is forward looking; turning back is not faith but unbelief.

Going Forward

The third choice is to go forward. Once this choice is decided upon the believer is confronted with a critical decision. Here is the center of the crossroad. One arrives at this
point by trying every way out and coming up empty. The
old ways no longer work and no new ways have opened up
the path. The Christian pilgrim is roadblocked with the
knowledge that turning back is deadly to faith, so is staying
put. Going forward is the right choice.

Destructive detours.—A word of caution is necessary
here. Sometimes in trying to find a new way out of crisis the
pilgrim runs down blind alleys. Neither staying still nor
turning back to old ways, the believer may take destructive
turns in an effort to move ahead. Both physical and mental
illness often result from these detours.[9]

A few years ago on a visit to my home, my father, Charles
Allen, asked to speak with me privately. He told me he was
constantly wrestling with the desire to kill himself. I was
stunned. My dad is a solid Christian layman. He had never
hinted to me or anyone else of his inner pain.

Talking things over we began to see that he was at a spiritual crossroad. He had begun a prison ministry to the local
county jail in the last couple of years. In the prison he had
begun to see the gospel differently. Men he had always
avoided and detested became Christian brothers. On the
other hand, former Christian brothers and sisters, and my
father's own conscience, began to accuse him of breaking
church tradition. The inmates were not only criminals,
most were also black. My father's church is segregated. Ex-
convicts might gain fellowship, but only with the right skin

color. Under Charles's witness, prisoners born anew in Christ asked about baptism. They could not receive it in his community of believers, a community where he had prayed and worshiped for forty years. How was he, a Christian near seventy, to decide which way to go? This struggle, along with other circumstances, drove him to despair. He found himself in the darkness of depression, a blind alley leading toward death.

For as long as I could remember, my father had kept a loaded pistol in his nightstand. On the day he shared his suicidal urge, he told me he had been unable to keep that gun out of his thoughts day or night. He said he had sold it to a neighbor. Then he gave a telling remark. He said: "You know, I would go to the jail and think of that gun and realize I had kept it all these years for the sole purpose of killing the kind of folks I now share Christ with." Called to identify with a new set of brothers, the gun which had threatened them now threatened him.

Charles Allen came to recognize the dead-end nature of the detour he was on. He sought and received help from God, family, doctors, and Christian friends, but not before he suffered a heart attack under the strain. He has made his decision about going forward. Every week he still visits the prison and he still attends the segregated church, ministering to and among the broken in spirit at both places.

Feeling like you are going crazy is not a sure sign that you have left the Christian way. Psychiatric illness is not simply a conscious choice to escape spiritual crisis, but sometimes it is a destructive detour. I asked and gained my father's consent to tell this bit of personal history so that others who need help will have permission to seek it. No one had told him that it was OK to tell someone when you were depressed. No one had admitted that sometimes being authentically Christian is enough to drive you to the edge of despair, like Jesus at Gethsemane. Mental and emotional distress is no sin; refusing to admit you have lost direction is.

If in trying to go forward you have lost your way in a maze of mental, emotional, and spiritual confusion, share it with someone in heaven and on earth. God loves those who are lost and God's true children will understand how it feels.

Back on track.—If going forward is the thing to do, how does one go about it? How can the roadblocked spiritual traveler find a renewed sense of direction? The Christian traveler's inner direction finder is blocked in spiritual crisis. It is as if the compass by which we have charted our course no longer points to true magnetic north. This sometimes happens in navigation because some nearby magnetic metal has distorted the accuracy of the compass needle. At spiritual crossroads we find ourselves in need of a redirected compass, but are unable to correct the cause of the disturbance. Checking deep inside where the ability to know direction according to gospel principle occurs, a redirection must be found.[10]

Looking for a new direction does not imply that the directions of the past were wrong, but questions their fitness for the present. One description of growth in faith describes it as feeling something like shipwreck.[11] A ship on the open sea may have been ideal for one leg of the journey, but when it runs ashore and splinters the traveler needs to abandon it for a new vehicle so the journey can continue. The direction-finding equipment of the ship's compass may need to be replaced by a land map. The journey is the same, the destination unchanged, but the direction finder at the core of our efforts may need renewal at such crossroads. The loss of what we indentified as the secure expression of our belief causes fear, but love calls us onward in faith.

The Heart of the Matter
The direction for the Christian spiritual journey comes from the heart. The crucial question at the center of spiritual crossroads is this: Can you receive a new heart? In biblical language the heart is the central and controlling core of

the person. It is the inner compass, the map and direction finder of the true self.

The Old Testament word for heart is *leb* and is usually translated *kardia* in the New Testament. In the writings of Paul this same idea of the central core of the person was sometimes expressed by "mind," "spirit," or "inner man."[12] At one place or another Paul used each of these words to mean the source of one's sense of inner orientation. In spiritual crises we need our hearts renewed; that is the bottom line of the matter.

The theme of needing a new and pure center for spiritual life so that one may turn away from death and toward life with God is found in the Old Testament. With a deep desire to be set right, the poet of the fifty-first Psalm prayed: "Create in me a clean heart, O God, and put a new and right [or steadfast] spirit within me" (v. 10). God asked in Ezekiel, "Why will you die, O house of Israel?" (18:31). He warned them to get themselves a new heart and spirit, then He promised: "A new heart I will give you, and a new spirit I will put within you" (36:26).

Jesus was in agreement with the idea that we are as we think in our hearts (compare Prov. 23:7, KJV). He taught that we produce good or evil from our heart and promised that the pure in heart should see God (Luke 6:45; Matt. 5:8). Those who see the kingdom of God, Jesus told Nicodemus, are those who have the new birth of the spirit given by the Spirit (John 3:3,6).

This renewal of self is a part of the renewal of all creation which is the purpose of God (Rom. 8:22). The renewal born in the initial salvation experience is advanced at every spiritual crossroad and its final destination is the glory of God. Paul spoke of God constantly renewing this "new self" in His own image:

> You have put off the old self with its habits, and have put on the new self. This is the new being which God, its Creator, is constantly renewing in his own image, . . . to bring you to a

full knowledge of himself (Col. 3:9-10, GNB; compare Eph. 4:24).

The Christian pilgrim is not to be conformed to the present circumstance but is to be continually transformed by the Holy Spirit's renewal of the central control center of the self (Rom. 12:2).

According to the Bible, standing inside a spiritual crisis and deciding to go forward with a new heart, leaving the old self behind, is the center of spiritual crossroads. It is not just an individual matter, though it is vital for individual survival. It is also a part of the purpose of God that we should face shipwreck, struggle to the shore, and go onward as a part of the whole creation, gathered together under our high calling in Jesus Christ.

Seen in this light the particulars of the suffering we face at a specific crossroad become less important than the response we make to those special burdens we carry. The challenge is to grow, "forgetting what lies behind and straining forward to what lies ahead" (Phil. 3:13). Only the new creation counts for anything (Gal. 6:15).

This new creation looks like Jesus Christ. Christ is the image of the new heart which is being shaped in all who go through spiritual crossroads. Paul used the comparison of the old Adam and Christ, types of the old self and the new (Rom. 5:14). The image of the earthly Adam, right for its time, will be replaced by the image of Christ (1 Cor. 15:45). The walk in newness of life is put on track at baptism and will be completed at journey's end. This maturing process of spiritual growth has borne its firstfruits in Jesus Christ (Rom. 6:4; 1 Cor. 15:20-23).

Those standing directionless at spiritual crossroads can look to Jesus who has been where we are and has marked the path to God. The importance of Christ leading us through each crossroad in the Christian journey was made clear long ago by Irenaeus (AD *c*.130-*c*.200) in his five books *Against Heresies*. Christ, he said, recapitulated or retraveled the human way which had lost its direction with the very first human beings. Step by step He revised the map of human experience.[13] Through every crisis, both developmental and conditional, from birth to death, in perfect obedience, Jesus made His way unerringly toward God.[14] The cross was the final great turning point, and Jesus "by his obedience on a tree renewed what was done by disobedience in a tree [in Eden]."[15] Jesus has seen the inside shape of every spiritual crossroad we face and has marked a way out.

Surrender

The Christ-shaped heart is the internal director we need for exiting spiritual crossroads, but the Christian heart cannot be homemade and it cannot be bought. It must be given to us. Spiritual crises are crises which require resources outside the reach of the one in crisis. God, a spiritual reality beyond ourselves, is the source of direction for the Christian traveler. The new heart with its redirection comes as a gift from the Divine.

Jesus is the proof that that gift can be given, but how can we follow His way? Jesus may have been able to hear God clearly in every crisis, but we are not Jesus and our hearing is not so good. What, then, is our part in receiving new directions at spiritual crossroads?

The answer is surrender. Letting go is at the center of the Christian response to spiritual crisis and is the essential act in Christian growth. Jesus' full surrender to His Father's will is expressed in the last phrases of His prayer: "Not what I will, but what thou wilt" (Mark 14:36). There is found the secret of obedience even unto death on the cross and also the source of the exaltation of resurrection. Who we are as we enter a spiritual crisis must die so that who we may become can appear. The controlling self which finds itself out of control in spiritual crisis must be replaced with a new heart formed by the Holy Spirit. Our part in this process is the surrender of the old self.

A growth principle.—This is a principle true in the growth of all living things. The fragrant orange blossom is beautiful, but it must fall away so that the ripe fruit can grow in its place. The human infant is precious but in the natural order of things is replaced by the child and then the adult on the way to what we correctly call ripe old age. The old forms must pass away so that the journey can continue.

Surrender in the spiritual realm is not automatic. There is an important difference between spiritual growth and some other kinds of growth. Spiritual growth requires choice. Plants do not make choices about their growth. They move from stage to stage naturally and easily if the surrounding conditions are right. The orange blossom does not decide it is time to go, it falls without giving the consequences a thought. Christians at spiritual crossroads, on the other hand, do not so easily let go of the old self and receive a new heart. We must choose to let ourselves be changed if we are to go forward with a new heart.

We are like the trapeze artist who grips the swing firmly with both hands. Arcing away from the platform, her back turned to her partner on the other swing, she reaches a moment when she must either let go, somersault, and be caught by her helper or swing back, hanging securely to the bar in her hands. If the show is to go on, she will choose to surrender present security for a moment of risky flight before being seized by security of another kind. The moment of surrender in spiritual crossroads is like that. It is an instant of exchange, the known for the unknown, the seen for the unseen. It is the moment of choice for faith.

The two calls.—This choice is between a double calling existing within each spiritual crisis. Surrender is the only way out, but believers at crossroads feel pulled in different directions. This stage has similarities to the three options of standing still, turning back, or going forward discussed earlier.[16] At this point in the crisis the believer has decided to go forward, to receive a new inner center of direction, but the moment of releasing the old heart must come before the receiving of the new. The call to a new path conflicts with the security found in the old.

The call to resist life and growth is real. It is a calling to stay with the familiar, the known, the proven. Under the right conditions this impulse is healthy, but when circumstances change it can become destructive. Horses in burning barns must be forced out of their stalls. With flames all around them they will not leave their familiar, safe stalls on their own even if a way out is offered.

Ways which have provided spiritual security for us in the past become sinful if, at spiritual crossroads, we are tempted to permanently settle in them rather than continue the Christian pilgrimage. Peter, full of fear on the mount of transfiguration, thought that the time to stop his journey had come. He suggested building booths for Moses, Elijah, and Jesus. It was a mistake which, if carried out, would have left Peter alone on the mountain as Jesus continued His journey to the cross and resurrection (Mark 9:2-8).

The call forward is a calling to life and growth. The problem is that the surrender of the outworn good must be done before we can move forward to the better. We must go on in faith. The Christian's task is the surrender of the old in order to receive the gift of the new. The safe path around the dangerous falls cannot be taken until the raft is abandoned.

Fear of the unknown is the great menace to self-surrender. My wife and I once hiked into a primitive wilderness area to visit friends in a fire tower. The trail was sometimes vague and we had only a hand-drawn map to follow. As the day wore on we often wondered if we had taken a wrong turn.

We were torn between the desire to go over one more hill or around one more curve in hope of finding the tower and the urge to retrace our steps to the car before darkness caught us. If we had been on a familiar trail we would not have been afraid to commit ourselves.

The call to life is always a call to a new trail. Though we desire to reach our goal, though we realize it means surrendering ourselves to the unfamiliar, we have a tendency within us to shrink back from the unknown. This differs from the first option to go back discussed in the last section because this is a desire to shrink back even after part of us has decided to go onward.

Here we see why the cross is crucial to spiritual crisis. It was at the cross that Jesus most clearly portrayed the essential of surrender. He let go of His life in obedience to God's calling forward. Suspended between earth and heaven, caught on a wooden cross, with no way to turn, Jesus surrendered His spirit to the One who had led Him into such dire circumstances (Mark 15:34; Luke 23:46).

Jesus' answer to the two callings was perfect trust in God, following God's call even to death on the cross. Through obedience in suffering He was made perfect, therefore God highly exalted Him and bestowed on Him the name which is above every name (Heb. 2:10; Phil. 2:10). He instructed all who wish to follow after Him to take up their cross daily, for those who would save their lives shall lose them, but those who lose their lives for Jesus' sake will save them (Luke 9:23). Like Jesus, we must surrender our lives at the crossroads in order to live for the journey home.

The divided heart.—Unlike Jesus, we do not respond to the double calling with perfect obedience but with a divided heart. The center of the self becomes of two minds. The inner compass wavers in its pointing. As in Paul's case, an inner war of opinions arise (Rom. 7:23).

This divided self must be converted to a unity of purpose

through submission to the Holy Spirit. The pure in heart shall see God (Matt. 5:8), and pure means simple, unmixed, one rather than two. On the inside of a spiritual crossroad, surrender is complicated by the problem of deciding which inner voice to obey.

If we make the wrong choice the result is stagnation, but even the right choice looks like death. In truth it is a sort of death. In spiritual crisis the choice is not between saving ourselves or losing ourselves; it is between surrendering ourselves for remolding in Christ's image or losing ourselves in futile attempts at self-preservation. Either way the old self will be no more. The choice is whether to lose ourselves in faith to the guiding Spirit or to lose ourselves to our past, immature ways; to be willing to give up control of ourselves or willfully remain as we are.

Jesus gave a one-line illustration of this odd connection between death and life. "Unless a grain of wheat falls into the earth and dies, it remains alone; but if it dies, it bears much fruit" (John 12:24). Imagine that grain of fruit deciding not to fall to earth but clinging to the security of the stalk at all costs and you have an accurate image of those at spiritual crossroads blocking their final fruitfulness.

The Holy Spirit is active in helping us make the choice to surrender our old selves for new life. The gift of discernment is the Spirit's acting within us as a kind of unbuilder. David Griebner wrote a story about a builder who went on a long journey to see a king. His progress was very slow for he spent so much time constructing and remodeling shelters for himself along the way. The king sent an unbuilder to help him along. This unbuilder's job was to persuade the builder to leave his shelters and continue the journey, trusting that his needs would be cared for. The shelters continued to be needed and built, but the unbuilder provided the discernment needed to know when to leave them.[17] The Holy Spirit meets us at spiritual crossroads where we hesitate to leave the familiar and coaxes us to move a little closer to our permanent home. The moment we completely let go the rebuilding of our hearts begins.

Application

Let us review some of the common landmarks of spiritual crossroads discovered in this inspection of the inside of a spiritual crisis. First, if you find yourself at a turning point in faith, you face three options: to remain where you are, to turn back, or to choose to go forward into the unknown.

Review your situation by looking back over the time you have been dealing with a particular crisis. See if your responses to your trial over time have produced any progress. If the answer is no, if the answer is that you have resorted to solutions that seem less and less likely to direct you toward the goal of Christian maturity, then recognize the danger of remaining in such a vulnerable spot or of turning back.

If you are at a genuine spiritual crossroad the answer to the roadblock in your faith is renewed direction from a transformed heart. The acceptance of this possibility is based on trust and faith in a loving God: trust that there is help beyond human imagining, faith that this help is in the hands of a loving God. When your direction fails, seek guidance from the creator of new hearts.

Surrender is our part in continuing spiritual growth by way of a transformed heart. The former stage must pass in order for the future possibility to be realized. This is a growth principle demonstrated among all living things, including living faith. You must be willing to be detached from the old forms so that new paths can be created.

Recognize that this will not come naturally in most cases. The word *secure* is formed from two Latin roots which mean free from care. What is natural at spiritual crossroads is a tendency to cling to past expressions of security even when they are no longer means that presently free us from our cares. You, the believer, are required to make a choice about where your true security lies.

This choice will be made between two callings: one toward surrender and growth, and the other toward shrinking back and failure. Face your fear of the unknown, remember that from Abraham's call to go he knew not where, to the grumbling by the Hebrews in the wilderness under Moses, to Mary's trembling before the angel, to your own struggles, the call to faith has been and is a time of sweaty palms and a queasy stomach. Think on Jesus who has been where you are and came out whole on the other side by placing His destiny in the hands of heaven. His cross is the sign of hope as you hang suspended within your own crossroad.

Finally, after you have recognized your crossroad for what it is and have chosen both to reject turning back and to accept the calling to renewal through surrender, be prepared to face a divided heart. Knowing what is going on and what needs to happen does not make those things occur. Wisdom is knowing that what we know is not what saves us. We can know what we need to do and yet remain unable to do it. Even the action of surrendering ourselves to God is a gift of the Spirit who unbuilds our false securities and leads us onward. To surrender is to quit trying on our own and then to surrender even our quitting to the Spirit—to quit quitting.[18]

We will return again and again in the chapters ahead to this mysterious and graceful act of surrender. One chapter will discuss common obstacles to spiritual surrender and another will take a look at time-honored biblical preparations for surrendering to the Spirit. For now let us finish the present up-close inspection of spiritual crossroads; it is time to search for the exit.

Exit to the Other Side

Spiritual crossroads are entered, endured, and exited. What does the other side look like? Persons just out of a crisis are like those who have turned at an unmarked intersection onto a new road and are looking for a highway marker to confirm that they are on the right course. How do you know you have come out of a spiritual crisis on the right branch of the trail and are not exploring some promising-looking dead end?

You know by the destination your travel tends toward. In the image of spiritual life as growth the goal is the fruit to be harvested. You know you are growing in the right direction by the fruit being produced. When Jesus was accused of being led by Beelzebul rather than the Spirit of God, Jesus suggested proof by fruit. Good trees do not bear bad fruit, and bad trees do not yield good fruit (Matt. 12:33). Grapes do not come from thorns nor figs from thistles (7:16).

The Fruit of the Spirit

The Holy Spirit creates the transformed heart, giving redirection to roadblocked faith; the redirection is always in line with the Spirit which produces it. The harvest of spiritual growth is the perfect fruit of the Spirit. As we emerge from a spiritual crossroad we will be moving closer to becoming the mature fruit of the Spirit of God.

Paul described the fruit of the Spirit in Galatians 5:22-23: "But the fruit of the Spirit is love, joy, peace, patience, kindness, goodness, faithfulness, gentleness, self-control." Notice that Paul wrote of "fruit" (singular) and not "fruits" (plural). This is not the gifts of the Spirit which are powers to do certain works and are variously distributed from person to person (1 Cor. 12:4-11). This is the one harvest to which all Christians are moving, described by a list of virtues it possesses.[19] If we have undergone a Christlike change in spiritual direction, that change will tend in us to produce a character of love, joy, peace, etc. These are signs of the Spirit bearing witness with our spirit that we are growing up children of God (Rom. 8:16).

We will not be fully loving or gentle or good. We are not mature yet, but the changes in our spiritual makeup will tend in the direction of the perfect love, gentleness, and goodness of Christ.

Some Helpful Questions

No short, long, or even endless inventory could fully capture the mystery of the riches of God's purpose toward us in Christ. Paul did not give in two verses an exhaustive classification of a genuinely transformed spirit any more than in the verses above them he had given a complete list of the works of the flesh (compare Gal. 5:19-21). Attempts to take each word in the list and unfold its meaning are valuable, but we should not overlook the unbreakable unity of the life being described.

Centuries of Christian commentary on genuine spiritual experience aid us in seeing the full depth of Paul's inspired description. Christian devotional classics are an excellent source of wisdom for judging the authenticity of chosen faith paths.[20] Recent writings also contain application of these landmarks of true faith in areas such as ministry to the sick, Christian doctrine, and discipleship.[21]

Each person's experience is different. No set of standards will apply to every person and no person's experience should be expected to fit all the marks. Certain characteristics do appear consistently, however. The simple questions that follow are developed from those constants. Asking them may help believers decide if they are on the right path.

How are you feeling?—While much emotion is no proof of true spiritual experience, the absence of emotional change is a sure sign of false religion.[22] Mind and will separated from feeling are as useless as driver and car without fuel. Upon exiting from a spiritual crossroad check your feelings, discerning their direction. If they turn toward peace, joy, and love, you are more likely to be on the Christian pilgrimage. Fear, regret, sadness, and hatred are signposts of another way.

Those who love are nearing God for God is love (1 John 4:8). Some say God's love is action, not feeling. They are partly right. God's love is always active, but it begins in a gut-level feeling.[23] It is always inseparable from compassion which means "with suffering (com + passion)." God's love is a sharing of the suffering of others; our cares become His cares (1 Pet. 5:7, KJV). The ultimate expression of this is seen in Jesus' last days in Jerusalem, the passion narratives of the Gospels.

Those who have experienced genuine Christian growth during a spiritual crossroad will emerge with a love which drives them to act on behalf of others who suffer. No commentary on this love surpasses 1 Corinthians 13.

Love is accompanied by peace. It is not a peace which is a result of blindness to the facts. It is not the blissful ignorance a drugged stupor may bring for a time. The peace of the Christian with a renewed heart is realistic and deep, found not by overlooking difficulty but by being given the faith to look through it to the other side. It is a taste of the Old Testament *shalom*, the intended unity and balance of all in relationship with God. This is not the peace of the world, an absence of disturbance, but the peace which Jesus left with us that our hearts might not be troubled or afraid (John 14:27).

Think of Jesus' disciples as described in John 20:19-25. They were huddled together behind locked doors, fearing the destruction that had visited Jesus on the cross might come for them next. Jesus appeared among them and said: "'Peace be with you.'" Then He showed them the bloody signs of Roman execution in His hands and side. Now those

were not exhibits one might ordinarily expect to ease persecution anxiety! The disciples, however, reacted with glad-
ness, and Jesus once more said: "'Peace be with you.'" This
was peace found at the crucial turning point of the cross; it
was peace from beyond the grave; it was peace beyond the
reach of human grasping. It is peace which passes all understanding, but keeps our hearts and minds pointing to Christ
Jesus (Phil. 4:7).

Joy as gratitude is a partner with the love and peace
which marks the exit to crossroads in Christian growth.
Thanksgiving, the Greek *eucharistia*, is an expression of joy,
chara. Luke 17:11-19 tells the story of ten lepers who were
healed by Jesus. Only one returned giving thanks. This act
of faith was heightened by the fact that the one healed was a
despised Samaritan. Jesus recognized this act of "re-joi-
cing" as a sure sign of true faith. Those who are rooted in
Christ abound in thanksgiving (Col. 2:6-7). The Lord's
Supper, the principal act of worship reaffirming the believer's oneness with Christ, was called by early Christians the
Eucharist, the thanksgiving, after Jesus' example (1 Cor.
11:24).[24] How do you feel: loving, peaceful, joyful?

So what do you think?—Feeling which is undisciplined
by thought is flabby sentimentality. Thought as well as feeling is altered by a successful passage through a spiritual
crossroad. By thought we build logical explanations of the
facts, we order and bring harmony to our world. The way
we think of God, ourselves, and others is changed by journeying through spiritual crossroads. Acceptable thought
patterns at one stage must be put away at another as one
travels to maturity (1 Cor. 13:11). The melody of life may
remain the same, but after spiritual crises the notes on the
staff are rearranged to deepen and enrich the harmony.

This change is in the direction of Christian humility, the
virtue of knowing where we truly stand under God. What
do you think of God? Spiritual crossroads point out clearly
our complete dependence upon God. Humility is a result of

this mature dependence. The thoughts of one who is on the right path after spiritual crisis are more God-centered, less self-centered. If we have been delivered from spiritual crisis by the Spirit's renewal, we know that without God's gift we would be stranded. We think highly of God.

Be careful, thinking highly of God is not the same as being swamped with religious thoughts. Just as the quantity of emotion in religious experience is no evidence of the genuiness of faith, the quantity of religious ideas and talk in a person's life is not evidence that the person is on the Christian way. Psychiatric wards are full of God talk, and though this is a sign of the importance of the spiritual in human health, the quality of religious thinking matters more than its quantity. Jesus' strongest criticism fell upon the most religious folk of His day. None were more occupied by religious concerns than the Pharisees. They even troubled themselves to tithe from their tiny herb gardens, but Jesus was more interested in the order of their concerns than the number of them (Matt. 23:23-24).

What do you think of yourself? Being humble means getting yourself off your hands. It is the opposite of pride. Putting God at the center of our lives means letting ourselves be placed somewhere else. Otherwise God becomes a means to indulge the self rather than the end to which our journey leads. An old joke tells of a drug addict's testimony which went like this: "Drugs used to be number one in my life until I met God; now God is number one, drugs are number two." Lifting up God is no sign of right direction if it is done as simply another means of self-satisfaction.

Some place themselves too high in the order of things. Just after calling upon Christians to allow themselves to be transformed and renewed in the direction of God's will, Paul told them to think straight (Rom. 12:3). Using the measure of faith they had been given, making a careful judgment, they were not to think too highly of themselves.

Some think too lowly of themselves. Beware of false humility. The opposite of prideful self-love is not self-loathing, but realistic love of self for God's sake. Thinking of ourselves too highly or too lowly are both ways of centering our thoughts on ourselves. Martin Luther in his misery could think of nothing but his own sinfulness. At the insistence of his spiritual director he became a teacher, preacher, and counselor. The director hoped some hard work would lift Luther's fascination with his own sinfulness.[25] "'You shall never wash my feet,'" Peter told Jesus in John 13:8. His false humility caused him to refuse at first to accept Jesus' service to him.

What do you think of others? The journey of faith calls us into community, not out of it. If we are on the path to Christian maturity we find our ties to others being strengthened. The Christian way is a way of at-one-ment, not division and separation. On the far side of spiritual crossroads we find ourselves "entrusted . . . with the message of reconciliation" (2 Cor. 5:19). Genuine spiritual crossroads put us on the road toward others.

Humility toward others is a sign of genuine spiritual experience. Humility is not clearly distinguished in the New Testament from gentleness and meekness.[26] Gentleness and meekness are character traits of one who has learned to live humbly with others. If God is at the center of our lives, and we know ourselves to be renewed in God's image, then we recognize that our brothers and sisters are also God's creation. We then think of our neighbors with respect as the gentlewomen and gentlemen that they are. This is not prissy politeness but the ancient honor and regard shown between persons of authority and nobility. When we think of others as sons and daughters of God and treat them accordingly, it is a sign that we are on the road to Christian maturity. What do you think of others?

What do you think of the world? God is not just drawing

you and me to our final destination. The whole of creation is caught up in this journey to wholeness. A sign of genuine spiritual experience, true Christian humility is a thoughtful grasp of the oneness of all creation: "For God so loved **the world** he gave" (John 3:16); "in Christ God was reconciling **the world** to himself" (2 Cor. 5:19). The whole creation, like a woman in labor, is groaning as it awaits the new creation of the Spirit (Rom. 8:22). Identification with the humus, the earth, is a sign of true humility. What we think of the air, the water, and our fellow creatures is a mark of our spiritual maturity.

Now what are you going to do?—Loving action is a mark of Christian growth. Christian maturity is shown in deed as well as in word (1 John 3:18). Those who talk the talk of Jesus should also walk His walk (2:6). Remember the parable of the two sons? Both were asked by their father to go to work. One said he would not, but did; the other said he would, but did not (Matt. 21:28-32). The one who did the job heard the father and followed him. Jesus revealed that actions are a mark of spiritual maturity. Those who exit spiritual crossroads find themselves acting differently, more like Jesus.

Carefully examine your actions. How do they compare with Jesus' ministry among the poor, the captive, the sick, the oppressed? The Sermon on the Mount in Matthew 5—8 is a good checklist. A note of caution: feeling good about such works and knowing what they are is not doing them. The question here is not whether your crises make you more sympathetic to other sufferers, or better informed about the facts of suffering; it is whether you move to relieve such suffering in others.

In assessing this area of Christian growth we do not study our prayer journals or read theology books for correct doctrine. We reread our calendars and recheck our checkbooks. How we spend our time and money is an accurate indicator

of the direction our lives are taking. After a spiritual crossroad both of these areas of life should show some transformation.

Christian action is not a matter of seeing the right and
doing it by force of character. Indeed, a peculiarity of the
pilgrims in Matthew 25 who had finished their journeys and
were about to receive homesteads in heaven was their surprise that they had been doing the right things. They did not
remember feeding, clothing, or visiting the hungry, naked,
imprisoned Lord. The sign of Christian maturity in works is
a growing naturalness about the right actions. Homing pigeons do not fly home because they are taught to, they fly
home because they are homing pigeons. Fully mature Christians do not act Christlike because they are following the
rules, they act Christlike because that is what they are.
Through spiritual crossroads the Holy Spirit forms within us
a clearer and clearer homing instinct for Christian action.

Conclusion

Up close spiritual crossroads reveal themselves as an entry, an interior of decision, and an exit. The entry is formed
by difficulties that resist solution by the usual means. Crises
grow as our usual ways of getting through them fail. The
center of a spiritual crossroad is the decision time in which
the pilgrim answers either the call to the old way of self or
the call forward to a renewed heart given by the Holy Spirit.
The traveler's part in renewal is self-surrender. Once this
surrender has been made the Spirit begins leading the believer into a new way of feeling, thinking, and acting which
are all more fully in line with the fruit of the Spirit.

Jesus' experience on the cross is our guide through these
crossroads. As His options became narrower and narrower
on the journey to crucifixion, He continued to follow in full
obedience the narrow path. His full self-surrender was demonstrated at the Garden of Gethsemane. From there He

went to His death and was raised to new life, the first fruits of God's eternal purpose for all creation. Each spiritual crossroad an individual travels through is a movement toward the great harvest of that purpose. Jesus' death at the crucial crossroads of Golgotha has cleared and marked the path for all who daily take up their own cross and follow Him.

Notes

1. Evelyn Eaton Whitehead and James D. Whitehead, *Christian Life Patterns* (Garden City: Doubleday and Company, 1979), pp. 50-53, examine adult crisis as entry, duration, and resolution.

2. See John Bunyan's classic, *The Pilgrim's Progress* (1676; rpt. Grand Rapids: Zondervan Publishing House, 1967), pp. 20-21 and 107-111.

3. See Roland Bainton, *Here I Stand* (New York: Mentor Books, 1950), pp. 27-28. For a dramatic sermonic treatment of Luther's struggle see Bill J. Leonard, *Word of God Across the Ages* (Nashville: Broadman Press, 1981), pp. 34-41.

4. Bainton, p. 34.

5. See the discussion of *peirazo*, chapter 2.

6. Bainton, p. 31.

7. See chapter 2.

8. Lewis Sherrill, *The Struggle of the Soul* (New York: The Macmillan Publishing Co., Inc., 1951), pp. 30-31.

9. See Anton Boisen's autobiography, *Out of the Depths* (New York: Harper and Row, 1960). Boisen was the father of modern pastoral care. His deep spiritual insights began in a spiritual crisis which included a psychotic break with reality.

10. See discussion of discernment in chapter 1.

11. Sharon Parks, *The Critical Years* (San Francisco: Harper & Row, 1986), p. 24.

12. John Knox, "Romans," *The Interpreter's Bible*, Vol. 9 (New York: Abingdon Press, 1954), p. 502; see also J. Behm, *"kardia," Theological Dictionary of the New Testament*, Gerhard Kittel and Gerhard Friedrich, eds., abridged in one volume and trans. by Geoffrey W. Bromiley (Grand Rapids: William B. Eerdmans Publishing Co., 1985), pp. 415-16. Evelyn Underhill, in her classic *Mysticism* (New York: E. P. Dutton, 1911), pp. 71-72, gives the following definition: "By the word *heart*, of course we mean not merely 'the seat of the affections,' 'the organ of tender emotion,' and the like: but rather the inmost sanctuary of personal being, the deep root of its love and will, the very source of its energy and life."

13. On recapitulation see Van A. Harvey, *A Handbook of Theological Terms* (New York: The Macmillan Publishing Co., Inc., 1964), p. 201.

14. See discussion of obedience as hearing and discerning God's directions, chapter 2.

15. Irenaeus quoted by Geoffrey W. Bromiley in *Historical Theology: An Introduction* (Grand Rapids: William B. Eerdmans Publishing Co., 1978), p. 23.

16. See Bonnie Lee Hood, "Spiritual Emergencies: Understanding Transpersonal Crises" (Ed.D. dissertation, The University of Massachusetts, 1986). She outlines a pattern of double surrender in spiritual crises.

17. David M. Griebner, "The Carpenter and the Unbuilder," *Weavings*, 2 (1987), 24-27.

18. On this paradoxical dynamic of the spiritual life see Edward E. Thornton, *Being Transformed: An Inner Way of Spiritual Growth* (Philadelphia: Westminster Press, 1984), pp. 106-107.

19. George S. Duncan, *The Epistle of Paul to the Galatians* (New York: Harper and Brothers Publishers [n.d.]), p. 173. For a diagram of the relations between the practice of the gifts and the spiritual reward of the fruit, see Benedict J. Groeschel, *Spiritual Passages* (New York: Crossroad, 1984), p. 168.

20. See E. Glenn Hinson, *Seekers After Mature Faith: A Historical Introduction to the Classics of Christian Devotion* (Waco: Word Books, 1968); for those interested in further reading I suggest the series, "Classics of Western Spirituality," by Crossroad Press.

21. See Rachel Julian, "Spiritual Discernment in Psychiatric Patients," *Journal of Religion and Health*, Vol. 26 (summer 1987), 125-130, whose concise summary was especially helpful to me in writing this section; see also Gerald G. May, *Care of Mind/Care of Spirit* (San Francisco: Harper and Row, 1982), and Richard J. Foster, *Celebration of Discipline* (San Francisco: Harper and Row, 1978).

22. Jonathan Edwards (1703-1758), Puritan theologian and revivalist, presents a clear argument for this in his *Treatise on Religious Affections* (1746).

23. "Compassion" in the Greek is *splagchnizomai*, "to be moved in one's gut."

24. See Richard A. Muller, *Dictionary of Latin and Greek Theological Terms* (Grand Rapids: Baker Book House, 1985), p. 106.

25. Bainton, p. 45. It worked, Luther turned to the Bible and found God's grace.

26. The eighth term in Paul's list of virtues in Galatians 5:22-23 is translated "gentleness" in the Revised Standard Version, "meekness" in the King James Version, and "humility" in the *Good News Bible*.

4

Crossroads:
Traveling Beyond Fairness

Though no two Christian journeys are the same, some spiritual crossroads are common to the experience of most believers. These crises are like major intersections where many roads converge. This chapter and the two which follow explore three frequent spiritual crossroads in the pilgrimage of faith. In the southeastern United States it is a common maxim that when you die, whether you go to paradise or perdition, you will have to change planes in Atlanta to get there. The three crises we will consider are nearly that busy in spiritual traffic. They are developmental spiritual crises which many Christians will face if the journey to maturity in this life continues long enough.

Many, but not all, will face them. Not every veteran Christian has been through each of these crises. Birth and growth are both part of the same cycle, but in the initial salvation experience the emphasis is on birth rather than growth. Not all who are born anew in Christ grow to the same level of spiritual maturity.

While salvation is not first and foremost a matter of growth, Christian discipleship is. By adoption through love my daughter is my child. Nothing else need be added to this bond. If she never grows through another stage in life's journey, she will still be my beloved daughter. In the new birth at salvation we have been adopted by God in love through Jesus Christ (Eph. 1:5, KJV). Nothing can separate us from the love of God in Christ Jesus, but our maturity is not guaranteed. For my daughter to remain forever an infant would be a tragedy; for Christians to remain forever immature is a greater tragedy still. Christians who remain immature are scolded in the New Testament (1 Cor. 3:1-3; Heb. 5:12-14). Not all Christians will face the same spiritual crossroads, but those who follow Christ toward maturity should not be surprised to cross paths along the way.

Those who seek to reach the goal of maturity in Christ are likely to travel through the crossroads leading beyond fairness, beyond tradition, and beyond personal understanding. These three turning points are common and recurring issues in the growth of Christians. Understanding where you are in regard to these main intersections can help you assess your progress and give you hope for the journey.

Let me hasten to say that this kind of reflection will not necessarily speed your progress. Knowing you are fifty miles from a certain crossroad will not exempt you from traveling that fifty miles, but it may make you more patient and less anxious during the journey. Knowing you are in a certain kind of crisis does not cause it to disappear, but it may make enduring it more possible and profitable.

The crossroads leading beyond fairness, tradition, and personal understanding were chosen for close inspection for three reasons. First, these three turning points in Christian faith are a source of much individual anxiety among Christians. Christians sometimes misunderstand each other because they are at different stages on the journey of faith. Finding out the differences in outlook on each side of these three common spiritual crossroads can ease anxiety within the believer and between believers.

Second, this diversity in outlook is also a source of tension within and between denominations. Reconciliation among Christian communities would be made easier if we understood some of the directions encouraged by communities of faith at crucial crossroads.

A third reason for choosing these three particular cross-roads is that each one clearly illustrates the way of Christian progress: growth through self-surrender in a personal encounter with God. This Divine-human encounter redirects life, molding our spirit more in line with the Holy Spirit.

Spiritual Crossroads and Faith Stages

We know that human personality grows by stages: infancy, childhood, adolescence, and so on. Developmental psychologists have done much to mark off the boundaries of these stages.[1] Physical, mental, emotional, and spiritual factors must be considered in this science of human development.

Faith also develops, for faith is bound up with the life of the believer. Our faith is related to our body, mind, and emotions. As these mature, so does our expression of faith. A three-year-old's faith cannot make adult commitments; the structures of thought and feeling are not ready for mature faith. Less obvious, but just as true, is the fact that we continue to mature in stages through our adult lives and so does our faith. Wisdom and faith are different in a mature eighty-year-old Christian than in a mature twenty-year-old.

Building upon and interacting with the findings of developmental psychology, persons such as James Fowler have added much to our knowledge of the stages that faith goes through as persons mature. Fowler has described six major stages in the Christian journey to maturity.[2] The spiritual crossroads which take us beyond fairness, tradition, and personal understanding were marked off by Fowler's survey of the spiritual journey.

These crossroads are transitions between stages of faith development, passages from one portion of the journey to another. We are dealing with the developmental crossroads discussed in chapter 2. These are the crises which occur as a part of the natural unfolding of human experience. Remember, however, that not every Christian automatically travels through every stage.

I have chosen to focus upon certain developmental spiritual crises because of their widespread appearance and influence on the faith journeys of Christians. Any conditional spiritual crisis which you meet will surely be affected and enlightened by where you stand in relation to these. Quite often the key to surrender and renewal in any spiritual crossroad revolves around one of the three issues I will address.

We must be careful not to view the stages of the spiritual journey as too rigid or frozen in pattern. Life is not a psychological theory and people do not move from one stage to another like walking up stairs. Spiritual crossroads may usually be faced in a certain order, they may often be found at certain ages; but do not be deceived by the averages. Faith occurs in the particular, in persons, and as individuals we are not nearly so predictable as we are in groups. Our redirected faith is a gift from the Spirit, not a human accomplishment. The Holy Spirit may usually give certain directions at certain ages in life, but no strict bounds can be put upon this movement of grace (John 3:8). The issues in the following chapters are characteristic of many spiritual journeys, but are not the only roads that lead home.[3]

The Call to Go Beyond Fairness

On the journey to Christian maturity we are called to go beyond fairness. For the remainder of this chapter we will look at the spiritual crossroad where this turning point takes place. It is an intersection between faith as fairness and faith as personal trust.

First let us look at what the Christian pilgrimage is like before entry into this spiritual crisis.[4] This leg of the Christian journey is dominated by fairness. The world believers travel through is simplistic, ordered along strict lines of good and evil.

All persons have needs and rights. Fairness is the give and take which allows each person's needs to be equally respected. The inner compass of the pilgrims guides them by pointing out right and wrong actions. Do right and you receive reward; do wrong and you are punished. After leaving the spiritual crossroad which calls us beyond fairness the truth within this view is not abolished, but "tit-for-tat" faith is no longer the guiding principle of the journey.

Those to whom fairness is the guiding principle understand the world through plain cause and effect. Right actions produce rewarding results; wrong actions produce woeful outcomes. The world is like an old cowboy movie in which the good guys all wear white hats and the bad guys wear black ones. The traveler can tell hat colors by simply noticing who obeys the rules. Little understanding of the depth of human motivations occurs on this part of the journey. Persons ask themselves if they are doing good or evil, but have little insight into why they do as they do. Nor do believers at this stage have much insight into the inner personal struggles of other persons. They judge them by outside actions, not by the heart's motivations.

God on this part of the journey is known as a strict authoritarian, like a law-enforcing judge, or an account-keeping banker. The purpose of the Ruler of heaven is to see that everyone gets a fair shake; the Divine Banker makes sure everyone's account balances.

God is related to in a rather distant, nonpersonal manner. Personal relationship language such as Father may be used, but the essential characteristic of God's place in faith is rewarder of the good and punisher of the evildoer. The Divine One is just and righteous and good, so the believer should be the same. Beware the wrath of God if you are not.

Progress in faith for those at this stage of the journey is accomplished mainly by figuring out what God expects and giving it. The Bible is read primarily as a lawbook, which if rightly understood will give the commands to live by if rewards are to be received. The moral of a text is its value. The full value of the good Samaritan parable, for example, might be exhausted in the moral that Christians should help those in need. The inner motivations of the characters and what that means for their relationship to God is overshadowed by the Golden Rule: "Do unto others as you would have them do unto you." Obey that requirement and God will bless.

Faith is what you do to get the right response from God. God's goodness is what God does to get the right response from you. Christian life is a contract for exchange of goods. Righteous mutual manipulation is the heart of the system. God made promises and can be held to them. If you do what you are asked to do, you have God over a barrel. The heavenly Fair Dealer cannot get out of the bargain agreed upon. You get what you pay for, but watch out, your debts will be settled one way or the other.

There is real strength to faith at this stage. Christians who do not recognize right from wrong are sure to lose their way in this world. Believers who do not embrace the Golden Rule have hardly taken the first step in the spiritual journey. This part of the trip to maturity builds a foundation of moral laws and ethical actions on which to grow in faith. These Christians seek to obey God, and they know where they stand.

There are also some real dangers. Faith as good works is a constant threat. If life is good and the journey easy, travelers are tempted to believe the progress being made is the result of actions they took, and not God. These actions may be crude animal sacrifice, required acts of penance, or charitable works. Even a denial of these and an affirmation of salvation by grace can become a work, if viewed as a cause which guarantees an effect. Any religious act may become a means to activate the system of divine rewards.

Another danger is loss of hope. Some who face crises believe that progress in faith is beyond possibility for them. Persons in times of tragedy who assume that you get what you deserve may believe themselves abandoned by God. "I must be doing something wrong," they believe, "or else God would not be punishing me so." Suffering can become equated with sin.

The experiences of life usually bring believers to a crossroad that calls them beyond faith as fairness. The spiritual crisis arises as the doctrine of fairness fails. Sooner or later the theory will not fit the facts; in life the innocent sometimes suffer. (Perhaps this last statement would be more accurate if the word *sometimes* were removed.) Unlike the old movies, the good guys do not always win.

More disturbing yet, none of us is a thoroughly good guy. Even those justified by grace through faith are, in Luther's words, *simul iustus et peccator*, "at once righteous and sinner." If we depend for spiritual growth upon the ability to go where the law of God points, we find ourselves unable to carry on because of two major obstacles: first, we cannot act right no matter how hard we try; and, second, even if we could there is no indication doing so would release us from suffering.

As the way narrows upon entrance into this crisis, we may try harder and harder to do what is right, only to find that the tragedy that threatens us is not relieved. We come to a roadblock: either God does not fairly give out rewards and punishments according to moral acts or God is not able to enforce the law. Either choice is a crisis in faith. A new direction must be found. God defined as law and order is not sufficient. The call in crisis is to surrender faith as primarily fairness and move on to faith as trust beyond reciprocity— good for good and evil for evil. We must allow the Holy Spirit to unbuild our secure structures of God as final fairness and find a new way to relate. The difficulty of this surrender is not evident until told in human experience. Let me demonstrate by a narrative from Scripture.

Crossroad in Uz

Perhaps the clearest biblical example of the crossroad calling us beyond fairness is given in the prologue to the story of Job, citizen of Uz. I do not pretend that the crisis of the call beyond fairness will explain the many-layered meaning of the Book of Job. My hope is that at one level the predicament of Job will illustrate the crisis.

The book begins with Job on the "fair is fair" road of faith. He was a blameless and upright person, fearing God and shunning evil. God is the witness to this (Job 1:8). In a fair world such good people should have good fortune, and straightway the fortune of Job is listed in terms of family and possessions. He was "the greatest of all the people of the east" (v. 4). Job not only did what it took to stay on good terms with God and society, he even performed insurance sacrifices to assure the good standing of his children before God, just in case they had sinned (v. 5). The road was smooth. The good Lord had blessed a deserving servant in a balanced world.

Then calamity struck. The hedge of protection and blessing that God had placed about Job was breached (v. 10). Job lost everything except his blamelessness and his uprightness. He lost his cattle, his servants, and even his beloved children to destruction and death. Soon he lost his health. His wife remained, and though she recognized his integrity, she counseled cynicism and suicide (2:9).

These things do not in themselves necessarily make for spiritual crisis. Bad things happen to bad people in a fair world. The problem was that bad things happened to a good person in Job's world. Two facts must be remembered. First, Job was not suffering for his sins. No less an authority than God had testified to Job's righteousness; and, even with the tragedies that hit him, Job did not lose his integrity. He continued to say and do the right things: "In all this Job did not sin or charge God with wrong" (1:22; compare 2:10).[5]

Second, God was somehow involved in the disasters and fatalities. It was God who put everything but Job's life into the cruel hands of the Adversary (1:12; 2:6). It was "The fire of God" which consumed his property and the "great wind" of the Creator which struck the house where Job's children feasted (1:16,19). It was God who was moved against Job, a person of integrity, "to destroy him without cause" (2:3). Job knew this. Twice he rightly recognized God as the one who had taken away that which comforted him, that which he loved (1:22; 2:10).

Job had followed God into a spiritual crossroad. He had lived a blameless life, yet things had not worked out for the good. Fairness did not fit the facts. Job had done his part in faithfulness; was suffering his payment? The part of Job's spiritual journey in which he could expect fair treatment, good for good and evil for evil, was over. Now which way did the road to spiritual maturity lead? The options seemed few and unattractive: curse God and die, or suffer in silence. Job was in need of a redirected faith, a new orientation toward God.

Now if you are like me, you find yourself wanting to help Job out of his bind. (Actually, we are more likely trying to keep ourselves out of that same bind.) First I like to backtrack Job's spiritual journey to see where he went astray. Surely there is a sin of his lying around somewhere. If I can just find it, a sense of justice at Job's trials will return. Also I will be warned to avoid the same mistake and can continue to travel life's road of fairness without worrying about suffering without cause.

The trouble is that I have to change the Bible to make an argument for Job's guilt. If God is for him, who can be against him? Yet Job, the innocent, suffers. Who can feel safe on a spiritual journey like that?

If blaming Job does not work, then I usually turn and blame the injustice on Satan. The devil made him do it. If Job is innocent and God is fair then that patently unfair character, Satan, must be at the bottom of this. The Adversary is the one who brought the subject of Job's persecution up, after all (1:11).

Two objections make this a dead end. First, as already documented, God is intimately involved in the destruction, as given evidence by both Job's and God's admission as well as the descriptions in the text. Second, even if Satan had done wrong, that does not ease Job's suffering or rescue Job from unfair treatment.

Few of us have completely put behind us the crossroad where faith turns beyond fairness. To the degree that you share my frustration with the question of fairness in the introduction to the Book of Job, you are experiencing or re-traveling this crossroad. Something has to be surrendered here. The old explanations will not fit. We need a new means of navigation. Should we turn back, saying, "God is obviously not fair or not ruler so why journey on to His kingdom"? Should we stay where we are, saying, "God is fair, I just can't figure out why in this case; I will settle down between my past understanding—now suspended by the facts—and some unknown explanation ahead, which I fear"? Can we risk letting go and going on?

We, like Job's friends, may feel slightly threatened by Job's plight and join his search for a solution (see Job 3—37). Standing at a distance watching Job try to get through his crossroad by wrestling with ill treatment is easy, however, compared to attempting to get beyond our own roadblocks. The anxiety, the disorientation, the grief is not appreciated until we ourselves face the loss of children, livelihood, or health, without apparent rhyme or reason. Then the question of fairness becomes real. As Christians we should look to Jesus for the answers.

Fairness and Following Jesus

The call to follow Jesus is a call beyond fairness. The Gospels tell of the rich young ruler (Mark 10:17-31; Matt. 19:16-30; Luke 18:18-30). His story is usually understood in terms of what it has to say about Christian attitudes toward material wealth. The moral is something like: beware of money, rich persons find it hard to obey the rule that they must give up their wealth to gain eternal life. This is a fair interpretation and true as far as it goes, but the encounter between the rich young ruler and Jesus takes place at a crossroad where believers are called beyond fairness.

The rich young ruler was on the right track. He was seeking eternal life. He wanted to know from Jesus what he had to do to get there. Jesus listed some commandments that he should keep. The seeker affirmed that he had kept them, yet he sensed that he lacked something. Jesus gave him one more rule to obey: "sell, . . . give, . . . and come, follow me." The young believer, so close to a new stage of the journey, turned back and went another way.

Like Job, the rich young ruler was not roadblocked because he was bad. The Gospels present him as good. There is no indication that he was a scheming hypocrite, On the contrary, Mark's Gospel hints otherwise, saying Jesus looked on him with love (10:21), and all three agree that he lacked only one thing in reaching his goal. His problem was not blind self-righteousness. The fact that he came to Jesus for help and his question about what he lacked (Matt. 19:20) show one who knows something is missing in his life.

What was missing? One answer is that he lacked the courage to obey the final rule, giving up his money. This is true but is not the whole story. Why could he not relinquish his wealth in exchange for a greater wealth, eternal life? Surely that would have been a more than even swap. Why would such a pious young property holder not trade securities of questionable and temporary value for long-term securities of inestimable value? The answer lies at the crossroad of spiritual growth which calls us beyond fairness.

The rich young ruler entered this crises through a sense of lack. He had long traveled the road of pleasing God by doing right. You name the law, he had kept it to the best of his ability. Like Job and Paul he seemed "as to righteousness under the law blameless" (Phil. 3:5-6), and his wealth was proof of his way's rewards. This way of fairness was not evil, it just was not adequate for the long haul. It became destructive when he decided to cling to it rather than surrender it and go forward in trust.

In facing Jesus, the ruler found a new directive: he was to give up his wealth and follow Jesus. Here he ended his journey, as far as we know. At the crossroad came a call to surrender. He could not heed it. The call was not just to obey one more command, make one more sacrifice to balance his heavenly account. It was also a call to give up accounting altogether, to quit adding up the bottom line. It was a call to faith beyond fairness.

The conversation Jesus had with his disciples just afterwards makes this clear (Mark 10:23-27; Matt. 19:23-26; cf. Luke 18:24-27). When told it would be easier for a camel to crawl through the eye of a needle than a rich person to get to the final destination, the disciples were more than a little astonished (Mark 10:26; Matt. 19:25). Why were they so surprised that the rich are not first-class travelers on the road to heaven? Simply put, they believed in faith as fairness. If the good get blessings because they follow the rules, then much wealth is a sign of much goodness. If those with the most evidence of merits in their spiritual accounts, people like the pious rich young ruler, could not get to heaven, who could? They betrayed this attitude: "Jesus, that's just not fair. You are putting the price of a ticket home out of reach." And they were right.

Now we can better understand the rich young ruler's sorrow. Jesus was not just asking him to give up his gold, Jesus was calling him to unbuild the counting house and to follow one who did not keep a tab on good works. The seeker was being called to quit the path of fairness, to surrender security in kept commandments, and to follow Jesus into unknown territory. He could not let go; he turned away, and his spiritual growth stopped at that crossroad, deaf to the call beyond fairness.

Peter's Spiritual Economics

Money was the first but not the main matter in this encounter. Peter's response proved that (Matt. 19:27-30; Mark 10:28-31; Luke 18:28-30). Peter was quick. He saw that Jesus was changing the rules. Having money was no longer the sign of a healthy heavenly account, giving it away was! Peter did a little quick calculating and began to feel pretty well off. After all he and the others had "left everything and followed [Jesus]" (Mark 10:28). He presented Jesus with the figures, asking what Jesus thought they would be worth upon maturity. The Master told him he would get a healthy return on his investment.[6]

If the one thing the rich young ruler lacked was following one more rule—the one calling for the sacrifice of his money—then Peter was right. The economy of fairness was the guiding principle of the spiritual life. The currency might change from getting to giving, but the system was the same. You got what you deserved.

Jesus did not totally reject this interpretation of the spiritual journey. Moral discipline and personal sacrifice were worthy goals, but they were not the worthiest goal. Both the rich young ruler and the disciples, including Peter, lacked something. They needed a renewed heart, a different direction for the next leg of the journey.

The rich young ruler was not prepared to accept what was in his view a bad bargain; Jesus was not eager, with Peter, to pay off a good one. Bargaining itself is to be left behind on the journey to Christian maturity. Jesus issued a call to the pilgrimage beyond fairness: "But many that are first will be last, and the last first" (Mark 10:31; Matt. 19:30). Keeping account of who gets what when is abandoned when we follow Jesus into maturity.

Another Way

To make the choice clear, Matthew added a parable which has plagued Sunday School teachers for centuries (Matt. 20:1-16).[7] A vineyard owner went out about six in the morning to hire farm workers. They contracted to work the day for a denarius, and set to it. The owner came back about nine and hired a second group, promising to pay them whatever was right. About noon and three in the afternoon he did the same. Then again, almost at sunset, he found another group of workers idle and sent them off to the fields without any agreed price at all.

When the day was over those hired last were paid first. Each one of them received a full day's pay, a denarius, even though they had missed eleven hours of work. Those who were hired first were pleased when they saw this for they thought they would receive more. They were wrong. When the first hired came to the pay table, they each received a day's pay, one denarius. Understandably disappointed, they grumbled that they, who had suffered the midday sun, were getting equal pay with folks who had put in only one hour. It was not fair.

The owner called them his friends but refused to up the ante. They got what they agreed on, he reminded them. It was his money and he could do with it as he pleased. He pleased to be generous and pay the last the same as the first. So much for fairness.

Why has this parable proven so frustrating to interpreters

and given birth to so many complicated explanations? For the same reason the first workers thought they would receive more than they had bargained for (Matt. 20:10). They thought fairness was the heart of faith. If the owner was fair and generous and good, then those who did more would get what they deserved, a bigger reward. He was fair, but he was more than fair. Those who worked in his service from the standpoint of fairness got exactly what they bargained for; those who came at it from a different direction got more than they deserved. Jesus is calling in the parable for believers to move beyond fairness.

The different direction, the "beyond" the parable points to is the surrender of faith as fairness for faith as personal trust. When students work for my family, we have to be careful. Sometimes when we try to pay them they refuse, offering their service free in the name of friendship. That is not fair. The difference between the first-hour farm workers and the last-hour workers was that the first-hour workers related to the owner by contract. Their relationship to him was one of agreement, so much work for so much pay. The sunset crowd related to him on the basis of personal trust. They worked for him without agreement as to reward, trusting him. They were what he invited the others to be: trusting friends, not business acquaintances (Matt. 20:13).

God is like the vineyard owner. Through Jesus God called the rich young ruler to surrender his life of adding up righteous actions, hoping someday to have enough to cash them in on a retirement home in heaven. To the disciples and Peter, God in Jesus gently affirmed their personal sacrifices but urged them to go further. Jesus tried to lead them to stop counting the cost and estimating the reward. The call was simply to follow Him.

The way of fairness was a beginning but would not take these believers the whole distance. Then who can hope to be saved? Trust me, Jesus said, only God can answer that question. Paul understood. In Romans 4:4-5 he wrote: "Now to one who works, his wages are not reckoned as a gift but as his due. And to one who does not work but trusts him who justifies the ungodly, his faith is reckoned as righteousness."

Present Company Not Excepted

What about us? If we live long enough we must face the facts, life is not fair. Often this truth appears as we encounter troubles that cannot be easily explained in simple terms of cause and consequence. If frustration is high enough or disappointment deep enough, we may find ourselves at a spiritual crossroad being called beyond fairness.

One of the most moving descriptions of such a crossroad came to me in the unlikely form of an exam answer. In a history class, I asked my students to discuss the ancient author or writing which had most changed or challenged their Christian thought. One young woman's answer revealed a spiritual journey at a crossroad. She wrote:

> This may be totally off base but I can't say that any one author or reading deeply changed or even challenged my Christian life this quarter. Although I have attended church all of my life until recently, I have never been faced with why I believed the way I did or for that matter what I believed. I do believe in God and I also believe that he watches over me. I pray every night for forgiveness of my sins and for the protection of my family but at the same time I wonder how such a wonderful, merciful God would let a very close family member suffer for a long time and finally die of cancer.
>
> The loss of that family member made me think more about Christian beliefs than authors or readings. Seeing the tape [which dramatized Martin Luther King, Jr.'s sermon, "Trumpet of Conscience"] also made me wonder why God would let people strive and die of so many sicknesses. Right now I am watching my granddaddy slowly lose his mind to Alzheimer's disease. I can't understand, myself, why God

would change such a strong, independent man into a helpless, wandering man.

I'm sure you've often wondered why I have such an ugly look on my face [during class discussions], but many times I have wondered why people would get so worked up for a God who allowed them to be destroyed or live sad lonely lives.

I guess the biggest challenge I have felt is having to face up to some of the thoughts I have about God. I don't want to sound like I don't believe or don't trust him, it is just very hard for me to be patient and understanding.

These were the words of a young Christian pilgrim roadblocked by the unfairness of life. She had entered this crossroad through a disturbing encounter with death and disease by way of the family member who died of cancer and her grandfather who had Alzheimer's. These personal tragedies had made her more aware of the suffering of the human race as a whole, and it all seemed unfair to her.

Her means of coping with difficulties was hinted at in her comments about prayer and church. She was, until recently, a regular churchgoer whose image of God was one who watched over her. Her prayers were for forgiveness of her wrong actions and pleas for protection of her family. Recently life's dangers had begun to challenge this way of traveling the journey of faith. The cruel illnesses faced by her loved ones had occurred despite her prayers and churchgoing. She had recently stopped the regular church-going and was questioning the character of the God to whom she prayed for justice, wondering how a merciful God could allow believers to be destroyed or to live sad, lonely lives. She continued her prayers, but with ever-decreasing patience and understanding.

The old ark of past securities was leaking and she was having to bail hard to keep it afloat. Her spiritual resources were narrowing. Her participation with a community of believers was becoming irregular. In a class where other students reacted with enthusiastic debate to the examples of great Christians of the past, she was unable to involve herself in the discussions. She approached God as a kind and generous person who would protect her, but the relationship was rather impersonal. It did not allow her to share directly with God her doubts or anger. These she had not even admitted to herself until recently.

Throughout our lives fairness is an issue. When facing tough problems, we should be aware of the fairness issue's power to alter our inner compasses or sway our heart's pure attention to God's will. Fairness, however, is not the overriding, guiding principle of most adult Christians. Fairness is usually discarded as the central map for spiritual growth during the teen years, except in certain Fundamentalist and Pentecostal communities where it is not taught as "a way station on a longer journey" but as "having the characteristics of a final destination."[8] This was the case with my student, and she felt trapped in a faith that was not working.

At this crossroad, she faced a choice: to hold on to an ever less secure and immature faith or to let go and trust the Holy Spirit to renew her heart in ways as yet unimaginable. Do not underestimate the challenge. She must surrender a stage of spiritual growth that she has lived within since childhood, a way which has offered her security and hope and a sense of certainty. Fairness is the glue holding her faith world together; to let it go is to submit to a world where rewards and punishments are not easily calculated. For her, giving up an image of God as fairness feels like giving up faith itself. Such is the call to surrender at each spiritual crossroad, a call to give up our half-grown images of God and to let them be replaced with the mature fruit of the Holy Spirit.

There is hope of an exit in her struggle. She is, at last, questioning her images of God and their adequacy. She has been able, indirectly through the exam, to share her doubts with another Christian. Perhaps she will be able to express those doubts to God directly in prayer. If so, this may open the way to a more personal encounter, an encounter offering insight into a wider range of personal responses to suffering, both within herself and within the heart of God. Perhaps she will be able to surrender the part of herself that sees God as no more than a judge offering pardons and protection. Then she might be drawn on the journey toward the God who in Jesus was neither pardoned nor protected, but who was personally caught up in the case of human suffering. As we shall see, this kind of personal encounter is characteristic of the next phase of spiritual growth which leads to a call beyond tradition.

My student friend is not alone. Most Christians are sometimes roadblocked by a gut-level demand that God treat us fairly, balancing reward and punishment, according to our understanding of those terms. We are called to surrender such demands and open ourselves to be guided beyond fairness. Buttrick's image of the witch of Alexandria, who carried a pitcher of water and a flaming torch, crying, "Would that I could quench hell with this water and burn heaven with this torch, so that men would love God for Himself alone," is calling to us if we are directed mainly by the desire for fair reward or fear of punishment.[9]

Long ago and faraway Job sat in Uz, suffering silently, waiting for a way out. Later and nearer, the rich young ruler refused to believe there was a better way than fairness. Still later, in the Garden across from the East Gate of the old city of Jerusalem, Jesus in spiritual crisis did not bargain for what was fair but surrendered Himself in personal trust to one He called "Abba." He did not avoid suffering. He did not seem to get what He deserved. He did receive what the rich young ruler longed for, and offers it to all who take up their cross and follow Him.

We are the present travelers of the road of faith. A compass reading is sometimes distorted by some nearby magnetic metal. At crossroads where the compass of fairness fails, ask yourself what evidence of your righteousness is distorting your orientation toward true Righteousness. Remember Jesus who blazed the trail you are on, surrendering even His innocent life in personal trust to a God He called "Daddy." Let us listen for the call out of crisis that will lead us beyond fairness.

Notes

1. See Erik H. Erikson, *The Life Cycle Completed: A Review* (New York: W. W. Norton & Co., 1982).

2. James W. Fowler, *Stages of Faith* (San Francisco: Harper and Row, 1981); see also James W. Fowler, *Becoming Adult, Becoming Christian* (San Francisco: Harper and Row, 1984); Thomas A. Droege, *Faith Passages and Patterns* (Philadelphia: Fortress Press, 1983).

3. For a discussion of the flexibility love and choice bring to faith development, see Gerald G. May, *Will and Spirit* (San Francisco: Harper and Row, 1982), pp. 168-69.

4. Though not a synopsis of the stages, the main points are taken from Fowler's description of the transition from Stage 2: Mythic-Literal faith to Stage 3: Synthetic-Conventional faith in *Stages of Faith*, pp. 135-50.

5. This is not a denial of the truth that all have sinned but a denial that Job's sins were the direct cause of his suffering. To do otherwise would contradict Scripture and lead to some unchristian approaches to human tragedy. Should we comfort all victims by advising them that blessing and suffering is directly proportional to sinfulness? Jesus did not (Matt. 5:45).

6. Notice that Mark alone reports in the fine print that persecutions are a part of the payoff (Mark 10:30).

7. See George A. Buttrick, *The Parables of Jesus* (1928; rpt. Grand Rapids: Baker Book House, 1973), pp. 158-65.

8. James W. Fowler, *Faith Development and Pastoral Care* (Philadelphia: Fortress Press, 1987), p. 85.

9. Buttrick, p. 163.

5

Crossroads:
Traveling Beyond Tradition

A second crossroad in spiritual growth common to mature Christians is the crossroad calling us beyond tradition. Many, perhaps most, believers never get beyond this turning point. Those who do find a genuinely personal faith and provide vital and thoughtful leadership for the church.

The Road Before the Crossroad

On part of the spiritual journey many find their way mainly by tradition.[1] Tradition is the beliefs and practices shared with us by trusted fellow travelers and accepted by us as our own. We travel this part of the road with the crowd, finding our way as our companions find theirs. We grow as much and as fast as the community will allow. We are dependent as at no other part of the trip upon the company of fellow believers.[2]

A Personal Journey with Friends

Our walk with God is understood at this time in person-to-person terms. Rather than the impersonal and distant figure of the fairness period, God is known as a more approachable friend or companion. Faith no longer seeks a fair reward from God, but moves us to be someone God will trust and like. God's affectionate approval is the reward we seek for it proves our self-worth. We want to become the Almighty's trusting and trusted friends because we prize above all else at this time the values of person-to-person contacts.

We chart our journey in this stage by relationships with other people. If we are being accepted by those we like and trust, we remain confident we are headed in the right direction. If trusted friends do not approve of our walk, we may doubt our own orientation and move quickly to get back in step with them. This is faith by reflection. Important friends act as mirrors for us: we see ourselves as others see us.

We also see God as others do. Though our relationship with God is personal and trusting, we test religious truth by tradition. Our view of what God is like comes mostly from those we rely on for spiritual help. We accept as true about God what our fellow travelers believe, discounting insights which are not part of the group view. We desire to stay in the mainstream, and the channel of faith is marked by the buoys of tradition. By the beliefs and practices of our trusted in-crowd we judge where the current of faith flows. We look to the markers of Christian tradition as set by reliable authorities to know where we are on the journey.

Outside Help

Our authority is mostly outside of us on this part of the journey toward maturity. Dan Aleshire called it the time of "E. F. Hutton faith," recalling the television commercials in which everyone stopped and listened when they heard: "Well, my broker is E. F. Hutton, and E. F. Hutton says. . . ."[3] True faith is defined at this time by the tradition given us by trusted persons we are loyal to. Thomas Droege titled this part of the spiritual walk, "I believe what the church believes," for the individual's faith is built from tradition supplied by the believing community to which she or he belongs.[4]

Believers at this stage are like Christian in Edmond Rostand's play *Cyrano de Bergerac*. Christian deeply loved Roxanne but expressed his desire through letters written by his friend Cyrano. Before the crossroad leading to travel beyond tradition, we sincerely and intensely love God, but we depend upon outside authorities to shape and express that faith. Even our image of the Beloved is drawn from our chosen tradition. It is as if Christian knew Roxanne only through what he heard from Cyrano, reserving no judgment of his own.

You might think of traditions as maps of spiritual territory. Different groups of travelers drew these maps. Each map showed areas of common agreement within one group. We accepted a particular map because we come to trust the group which made it. Deeply, personally committed to the journey of faith, we chart our position and course by the experiences of those who have gone before us revealed on the map of tradition. We may question the interpretation of certain details, but at this stage of the journey we never question the map itself.

The Advantages

The strengths at this stage of Christian maturity are great and are carried over into the rest of the journey. Faith is deep and personal, fired by a desire to be related to God in a feelingful way. This accent on the personal is also played out in the community of believers. Relationships with fellow travelers are treasured and sought. The New Testament ideal of Christian community begins to be practiced as we recognize our dependence upon other members of the body of Christ. A deep individual commitment to God and God's family is common to this part of the walk.

This stage is also a teachable moment. Desiring to meet fellow Christians' expectations, believers are sensitive and open to instruction. This is the best time to teach the basics of Christian faith, building a foundation of tried and true doctrine drawn from the cloud of witnesses which surround us (Heb. 12:1). Tradition gives a vocabulary to name the inner meaning of life's events.

The Dangers

For many churches and believers, this level in Christian growth is a final destination on the way to Christian fruitfulness. This is stopping short. Elements of immaturity remain. Mature faith is ultimately under the sole authority of the Holy Spirit. Believers who have not traveled beyond tradition find it difficult to distinguish their tradition from the leadership of the Spirit. In areas where these two differ the highest loyalty to the Spirit is at risk. If growth stops here believers may never act under God's authority alone, always tempering obedience with in-crowd approval.

Another danger is in the frailty of the outside authorities we place our trust in. When those identified with the right route to God prove false, we may believe God is false or draw back from following God in community. Many considered identical the leadership of the Holy Spirit and the directives of supposedly reliable "men of God." Their faith was wilted by the fall of certain idolized televangelists. How many Christians have given up the act of meeting together and encouraging one another because they were disappointed by fellow travelers they relied upon? At these crossroads we are called beyond tradition.

Coming to the Crossroad

We enter the crossroad calling us beyond tradition as life stretches beyond the breaking point of tradition's power to make sense of things. This happens because no religious tradition is God's view. God's vision is wider than that of any chosen in-crowd, no matter how trustworthy.

Questions and Answers

If something causes a clash between what the church believes and what the believer sees to be true, the description of God given by authoritative friends in faith is called into question. Most often this takes place as the believer leaves home, perhaps going into the military or off to college or taking a job transfer. It may occur as the believer weighs valid differences held by equally reliable authority figures such as a pastor and a parent. Either way, the believer sees maps that differ. These are maps of the same spiritual territory, but in important ways they do not fit the tradition the mover carries. The maps do not match and cannot be harmonized. Honest doubts about one's own personal faith in God arise, for at this stage personal faith is one with the map of tradition. These doubts are a first sign of the call to move beyond tradition.

When troubled by doubt, the believers' past solution was to find tradition's answer and to repeat it with sincerity. Answers were placed in their hands unexamined, accepted because they came from trusted authorities. If that can be done now, no spiritual crisis exists, and the journey continues on the same level as before. But passing out stock answers taken from the shelf of one's heritage without personal inspection can be embarrassing. This is the case when others offer a different option polished and prepared by thoughtful and personal consideration. The borrowed nature of the ingroup answer is more glaring if the persons offering the alternative prove to be as trustworthy as one's chosen authority figures.

Repeating the traditional answer with more feeling is a common response to the mounting crisis. If you become angry when comparing your map with the maps of others, you may be hearing a call to go beyond tradition. "Methinks they protest too much" is a fitting proverb for believers whose heat reveals a lack of light.

As the crisis continues to grow, believers become disoriented, at a loss to know where to look for direction. Their old direction finder, tradition, is failing, and they are not yet ready to trust a new authority. Thus they find themselves at a spiritual crossroad on the journey to Christian maturity.

The Surrender

The believer is called at this crossroad to surrender the armor of outside authority. Faith to this point has been protected by a defense built from tradition's answers to life's problems. Believers challenged by tough questions never let them into their hearts. They hid behind a shield of mutual tradition supplied by trusted authorities. This crossroad calls for the surrender of questionless faith. Faith secure only when troubling questions are ruled out is faith protected from real life, which asks such questions of us all.

This surrender is like learning to drive at a driving school. In training the students drive in a car with two sets of controls, one directed by the trainee and the other commanded by the instructor. Though the student sits in the driver's seat, whenever a problem arises the instructor takes over and steers them out of trouble. The route and speed are really controlled by the copilot. At the crossroad calling beyond tradition, we are to surrender the instructor's help and drive solo. Only then are we really free to go where we sense God leading us. Believing, like driving, may first be learned by mirroring the good example of others, but faith must become free to answer for itself the call of the Spirit within.

The Inner-Directed Heart

The call is to let the Holy Spirit create a renewed heart more inner directed than in-crowd directed. God's kingdom is bigger than any tradition's map. Mature Christians are called to correct their traditions by careful common sense applied to personal faith. When our tradition does not match faith's personal experience, we are to ask: Why? Thinking about faith, loving God with all our minds, is an important part of a mature guidance system. If given an answer more accurate than the map of our tradition, we are to redraw the map. Early Christians called this obeying God and not men (Acts 5:29). We are not required to discard our old map on this new stage of the journey, but to transform it, mapping out an ever more mature way under the guidance of the Spirit.

Movement through the crossroad to travel beyond tradition is like the development from a reflex to a chosen response. Infants are born with a grasping reflex. They automatically grip whatever is put into their hand. Within a few months this reflex is replaced by grasping which is deliberate. They choose to hold on or let go. Between the loss of the reflex and its replacement by voluntary grasping is a period in which children cannot hold on by reflex or by choice. This is frustrating for the babies and sometimes frightening to parents who do not understand this natural development. Tradition-bound believers reflexively take whatever is handed them by their trusted authorities. Through spiritual crisis they mature to the point of choosing and rejecting faith elements by an inner guide, but during the crisis they may feel faith is beyond their grasp altogether.[5] The movement beyond tradition is a difficult one.

Dead Ends and Outside Difficulties

Persons respond to this crisis in different ways. Many decide to live within one tradition and lock the doors to any others. They refuse to face any revealing questions. They simply disregard all challenges to their tradition, not allowing questions to be asked in an honest way. They are like some ministerial graduates who proudly proclaim their faith did not change one whit at school. They have reason to be proud; it takes a strong will to hold a mind shut for four years or so, but it can be done!

Others use different rules in different settings. They live by one tradition in one setting and by a different one in another. We generally call these folks hypocrites, Sunday Christians who act quite differently at church than they do at their jobs or in their homes. Dependent upon several in-crowds for direction, they never grasp faith for themselves.

They direct their lives by secondhand beliefs passed on by different sets of friends and authority figures.

A more mature choice is to surrender the old security of outside authority, living in patient trust until the redrawn tradition comes clear. Such surrender depends upon trusting God to guide us when our map fails. The tool by which the new path will be seen is our God-given plain reason. Upheld by the Spirit, we ask without fear which way is right and wait faithfully for an answer.

All the difficulties at this crossroad do not come from within us. The crossroad by which we travel beyond tradition is one which may bring conflict with many of our fellow travelers. Job, whose life and faith put the "fair is fair" tradition into question, became the target of his friend's condemnation (Job 22). Sadly, in-crowd navigators often see those outside their tradition not as believers with different maps, but as unbelievers. After all, tradition-bound Christians believe their tradition and genuine faith are the same thing.

The stress following God's call to leave the crowd is revealed in a question once asked of our old friend Martin Luther. Through thoughtful, personal study of the Scripture, Luther came to believe in salvation by faith alone. His beliefs were blasphemy to the religious authorities of his day. He was called by faith beyond the tradition in which he had been reared.

In the year 1519 Luther stood trial for his life, accused of heresy. A simple Catholic monk born of peasants, he stood before the Holy Roman Emperor in a great hall in the city of Worms. He was there to be interrogated by the Archbishop's representative, John Eck. Eck put a question which brings into sharp focus the challenge of the call beyond tradition:

> Martin, how can you assume that you are the only one to understand the sense of Scripture? Would you put your judgment above that of so many famous men and claim that you know more than they all? You have no right to call into

question the most holy orthodox faith, instituted by Christ
the perfect lawgiver, proclaimed throughout the world by
the apostles, sealed by the red blood of the martyrs, con-
firmed by the sacred councils, defined by the Church in
which all our fathers believed until death and gave to us as
an inheritance and which now we are forbidden by the pope
and the emperor to discuss lest there be no end of debate. I
ask you, Martin—answer candidly and without horns—do
you or do you not repudiate your books and the errors which
they contain?[6]

The elements of Luther's crossroad are plain. Through
prayer, reasoned Bible study, and personal experience, he
had come to question and reject some of the views of his
tradition. The outside authorities, given voice by Eck, saw
no difference between that tradition and "the most holy orthodox faith" itself. Honest questions were not even allowed
lest they cause endless debate. Luther's personal faith decisions were heresy because they did not agree with the in-
crowd. He was not asked to repudiate them because they
were not true but because they were not traditional. To his
persecutors God's truth and their tradition were equal.

Luther's physical life was at stake in his answer. More importantly, the growth of his spiritual life depended upon his
reply. Did he dare surrender dependence upon tradition and
trust God alone to lead in the right direction? Before we
hear Luther's answer, let us look to Scripture, the source of
his radical ideas.

Peter's Turning Beyond Tradition

Peter passed through the crossroad leading beyond tradition. His turning to follow the Christ revealed in Jesus rather
than the Christ expected by his tradition took place gradually over the years. We should not be surprised; the journey
through the crossroad calling us beyond tradition is a slow
one. As a rule it takes four to ten years to complete, if it

takes place at all.[7] The Bible's record of the events in Peter's life tell us much about his crisis at this crossroad.

What's in a Name?

At Caesarea Philippi, Jesus asked His disciples: "Who do men say that I am?" (Mark 8:27-30). They answered with what they had heard others say. Jesus was not satisfied. He called for a more personal response: "But who do you say that I am?" Peter had a personal answer. If he was right, confessing it aloud was to make the most important commitment possible; if he was wrong his very soul was at risk. He stepped courageously forward in faith. "You are the Christ," Peter boldly claimed. He was right. Jesus accepted Peter's confession, praising him in Matthew's account (Matt. 16:17-20). Then Jesus warned the disciples not to tell anyone.

The wisdom of Jesus' warning comes clear in the verses which follow (Mark 8:31-33). Jesus was the Christ or Messiah, but not the kind Peter wanted. Jewish tradition had taught Peter and the others to expect the Christ to be a military figure who would run the Romans out of Israel and set up an earthly political kingdom. Peter's tradition needed redirecting. Jesus immediately began the task. He taught His destiny of rejection and death at the hands of the authorities in Jerusalem. Jesus was remolding the Christ tradition in terms of a suffering servant, and He said so plainly.

Jesus stretched Peter's tradition of the Messiah beyond the breaking point. Peter's confession was true, but needed to grow. He personally and deeply believed in Jesus as the Christ, yet Peter's definition of Jesus' title came from Jewish tradition with no questions asked. Jesus challenged him to go beyond tradition's bounds. Peter was not ready. He took hold of Jesus and began to rebuke Him (v. 32).

Peter's outside authorities had given him an image of Christ drawn partly to human scale. When Jesus did not fit the image, Peter tried to trim Jesus down to size rather than revise tradition's model. God is never fully contained by religious tradition. The living Lord is the judge of our faith; our faith is not the measure of Christ. Jesus had heard Peter's suggested self-definition before, substituting strength for suffering and sovereignty for service. He had heard it during the wilderness temptations. Such suggestions were satanic distortions of the true path to God. "Get behind me, Satan!" He told Peter, "For you are not on the side of God, but of men" (v. 33). Peter was at a crossroad calling him beyond tradition.

Peter was trying to get to the Messiah by a map which was given him by his Jewish heritage. Following that way with confidence he made some marvelous discoveries. But when those discoveries beckoned him to areas that were not on his old and trusted Jewish map, he was troubled. He had to stop and decide whether the new way pointed out by Jesus was true. If it was, he must surrender his valuable but too narrow past for reformation. If not, he must turn back and go only to those places which his church could guide him. We know Peter's final answer. He used his own experience coupled with his beloved past community to map out new territory, the Christian church.

Obstacles of Overconfidence and Comparison

Let us listen in on another conversation between Jesus and Peter. This one is given to us in the Gospel of John, chapter 21. The resurrected Jesus met and had breakfast with the disciples on the seashore. After eating, Jesus and Peter took a stroll along the beach. Three times Jesus asked Peter if he loved Him; three times with feeling Peter answered yes.

These three confessions perhaps reminded Peter of three denials only a few days before (John 18:17,25-27). If so, Peter would have done well to recall that unquestioning certainty based on former understanding is no sign of spiritual maturity. Just before the denials Jesus told His disciples that they were not ready to follow His path. Peter disagreed: "Lord, why can I not follow you now? I will lay down my life for you" (John 13:36-37). Peter asked no questions of his traditional interpretation of Jesus' purpose and future.

At Jesus' arrest Peter was indeed ready to die. He pulled his sword and drew first blood from the band of soldiers and religious leaders who came to take Jesus away (John 18:1-11). Jesus rejected this violence, asking Peter: "Shall I not drink the cup which the Father has given me?" (v. 11). The Messiah was giving up to death before the fight even started. Peter withdrew. Peter had been ready to die for the fighting Messiah of his tradition, but he was not prepared to fight for the dying Christ Jesus. Again tradition betrayed Peter; again Jesus called him beyond tradition.

On the seashore, after the third confession of personal loyalty and love, Jesus predicted martyrdom for Peter, and said simply, "Follow me" (John 21:19). Peter looked around, saw another disciple following them, and asked, "Lord, what about this man?" (v. 22). Jesus sternly replied, "What is that to you? Follow me!" (v. 23).

Peter was still not ready to follow Jesus on his own. He was personally and sincerely attached to Jesus, he was loyal and true; but he was not ready to keep his eyes on Jesus alone. He still had to look around, comparing his walk to the walk of other believers. This need to put off following Jesus until we know how our commitment lines up with the other fellow's is a sign of immaturity. It is best left behind at the crossroad calling us beyond tradition.[8]

Jesus was calling Peter and calls us beyond tradition to discipleship based on God's inner authority. Not God as defined by others or God's treatment of others, but God directly leading through the living Spirit of Jesus in our hearts. Peter was growing, he was turning, but the crossroad was not yet left behind.

Acting Differently

The disciples, including Peter, formed a new community of faith in Jesus' name, the Christian church. According to Acts, this in-crowd of faithful believers lived within its Jewish heritage. They continued to worship at the Temple and observe the Jewish religious calendar, follow the Old Testament dietary laws, and require circumcision for salvation (Acts 2:46; 10:14; 15:1). This first Christian tradition was on the verge of being transformed, and Peter's personal spiritual crossroad played a key part in the change.

Acts 10 tells of another step in Peter's journey beyond tradition. One of the two main characters in this chapter is a Gentile named Cornelius. Gentile means non-Jew, and Cornelius certainly fit that description—he was a Roman soldier. Cornelius had become interested in the Jewish faith but had not yet converted. An angel appeared to him, telling him to send for Peter who was in a nearby town (Acts 10:1-9).

Peter is the other main figure in the chapter. The day after Cornelius heard from the angel, Peter also got a message from heaven. He was waiting for lunch when a vision appeared to him. In a sheet were many kinds of animals. A voice told Peter to kill and eat them, but he refused because some foods were sinful according to his tradition. The voice said that what God called clean, Peter should call clean. This exchange of command and refusal happened three times before the vision ended. Peter was mystified. Just then, Cornelius' messengers knocked at the gate, asking for Peter. The Holy Spirit advised the disciple to go with them (Acts 10:9-23).

Arriving at Cornelius's house, Peter admitted he had accepted the invitation only because God had shown him that he should not call persons outside his own religious tradition unclean (Acts 10:28). After a time of sharing, the Gentile Cornelius and his companions were filled with the Holy

Spirit and baptized in Jesus' name. Peter and the circumcised Christians were amazed "because the gift of the Holy
Spirit had been poured out even on the Gentiles" (v. 45).

Tradition was stretched at Caesarea Philippi, outside authority was challenged at the seashore, but Peter still was
not free from his traditional biases. He did not believe that
the Holy Spirit could be given to anyone outside of his circumcised Jewish in-crowd. Three visions from heaven and
proof in the conversion of Cornelius were necessary to
change his mind. Now not everyone requires three visions
and direct prophetic instruction from the Holy Spirit, but
none of us go through the crossroad leading beyond tradition easily. Most, like Peter, box God's activity within the
boundaries of the tradition in which we discovered the
Spirit at work. Even after we recognize this in our heads,
old habits are hard to break.

Acting Consistently

Peter's time at this crossroad was not yet complete. Paul
recounted in Galatians a confrontation with Peter. Peter and
Paul had both ministered to the non-Jewish Christians in
Galatia. Peter at first mixed freely there with those Gentiles
he had once considered unclean. The believer who once
refused non-Jewish food even when the Lord passed the
plate now ate at Gentile tables. Then one day some of Peter's
old in-crowd from Jerusalem showed up. He drew back
from his new Christian friends, segregating himself from
them to please his old circumcised chums (Gal. 2:11-13).
Paul's writing makes it possible for us to almost see Peter
hastily shoving back his chair and yanking off his napkin as
the Jerusalem bigwigs walk in. We can almost hear his apologies: "Don't get me wrong, guys. I don't make a regular
thing of this eating with Gentiles. I just happened by and sat
down for a minute. It won't happen again!" Paul "opposed
him to his face, because he stood condemned" (v. 11).

Peter still had not surrendered his heart fully to the inner direction of the Spirit. He was less tradition-bound than in the past, but he changed maps according to the crowd he was traveling with. Among the Gentile Christians he ignored the outgrown parts of his tradition, but when the external authority figures from Jerusalem showed up he turned his back on his newfound fellow travelers.

Contrast Peter's lane-changing with Paul's path in the same circumstance. In the letter to the Galatians, Paul argued for a gospel not directed by people, not even by the apostolic in-crowd, but by God (Gal. 1:10 to 2:21). Though all of the Jews followed Peter's lead, though even Paul's co-minister Barnabas was carried away by their influence, Paul was unwavering. He did not turn from the truth of the gospel as it had been revealed to him by Jesus Christ. He was following the inner direction of the Spirit beyond tradition (1:11-12). He had come through the crossroad, and at the time of the letter was calling the Galatians to follow.

Accepting the Consequences

On another occasion, Peter stood before a council of Christian authorities in Jerusalem which was also considering the relationship between Jewish tradition and Gentile Christians (Acts 15).[9] Paul and Barnabas had recently returned from Paul's first missionary journey, and were giving talks in the churches—without slide-show accompaniment—about the many Gentiles who had been saved (Acts 14:27-28). Some folk from Judea disrupted these meetings with the teaching: "'Unless you are circumcised according to the custom of Moses, you cannot be saved'" (Acts 15:1). In other words, if the converted Gentiles refused to follow the Jewish tradition, they were not saved Christians. The Antioch church sent Paul, Barnabas, and some of their friends to Jerusalem to settle the dispute.

Heated debate between the Antioch Christians and the

Jerusalem believers stirred the Jerusalem or Apostolic Council which considered this matter. Then Peter rose. He defended the view of the Christians from Antioch that the Holy Spirit within the heart is the crucial proof of Christian faith, not external tradition (Acts 15:7-11). The Council's decision was to offer a compromise: circumcision was not necessary for Gentile Christians, but they should nonetheless practice some lesser Jewish traditions (vv. 19-21). This compromise was acceptable to the majority, including Paul, Barnabas, and Peter.

Two things are noteworthy about Peter's participation in the Jerusalem Council. First, he gave evidence that he was moving out of the grip of traditions and the in-crowd influence. He was apparently in the minority among the Jerusalem Christians, yet he used his plain reason applied to personal experience to redraw the traditional lines.

Second, this turning beyond tradition probably cost him influence. Peter had been portrayed as the leader among the disciples since the early days of the ministry of Jesus. This continued through the early chapters of Acts. But as he followed the inner direction of the Spirit even when it meant confrontation with the in-group majority opinion, Peter's authority among the Jewish Christians waned. Judging by the biblical evidence, after the Jerusalem Council Peter never again exerted much influence within the inner circle of the Jerusalem Christians.[10] Though he lost immediate influence, the path Peter followed in traveling beyond tradition took the Christian gospel into all the world and down the highway of history.

Summary

Let us review some characteristics visible in Peter's life of a crossroad calling beyond tradition. At Caesarea Philippi Peter faced the hard work of separating tradition from the truth to which tradition points. His tradition gave Peter the name *Christ*, but Jesus called Peter to examine that term and understand its meaning. Before the crossroad calling us beyond tradition, believers do not consider the difference between what a religious symbol is and what it means. This would require questioning religious tradition's completeness and before this crossroad no questions are allowed. Peter knew who the Christ was before he knew what the Christ meant. The meaning of mature discipleship was slow in coming. Peter had to put his mind to it.

One reason the awakening came so slowly was Peter's certainty that he knew all the truth already. Only the tragedy of his denials while Jesus stood trial showed Peter he had much to learn. The Holy Spirit cannot lead us if we do not know that there is someplace else we need to go. Another reason for delayed redirection was Peter's need to compare himself with others. At the seashore, he was unable to follow Jesus without turning back to see if others would be coming along. What other people think or do should not be the clinching argument in disciples' decisions.

Even after these growth experiences, Peter found old habits hard to break. At first he tried to keep the past tradition by carrying it unchanged on his Christian walk. He was a Christian who kept the Jewish laws of separation from unclean persons. He was amazed when the Spirit led him to give up this segregated view of faith and placed him in the middle of a Spirit-filled group of Gentiles at Cornelius's house. We cannot keep faith by building a moat to separate us from those who do not keep our faith tradition in every respect.

Next Peter clung to tradition by obeying one set of authorities in one situation and another under different conditions. At Jerusalem he avoided Gentile table fellowship, but among the Galatians he ate with all Christians. Paul called his hand on this crooked witness to a straightforward gospel. The answer to the call beyond tradition is not a shift from one external authority to another. The call is to surrender final loyalty to the inner direction of the Spirit. From believing unquestioningly what the church believes, we are called to a belief aided by thoughtful understanding.

This spiritual crisis placed Peter at odds with his in-crowd. Under the guidance of the Spirit at the Jerusalem Council, he stood on the side of the minority, outside his past tradition. This redrawing of the majority map blocked his influence and reputation for a time but guided him to the way of the eternal for the long run. This loss of popularity is often a part of the surrender called for at the crossroad. From believing what the church believes without question we are called to believe as God gives us understanding.

The Crossroad in Our Lives

The crossroad calling beyond tradition confronted by Peter is still encountered by Christians today. I left my rural Alabama hometown in 1971, trusting Jesus in my heart. I was a good young Christian, but my Jesus was a Jesus of all-white churches. Those who had shared with me the good news of the new birth had done so within an all-white tradition.

I left home in 1971 to go to college. There I found a church where Jesus was preached, but this time the folks who followed Him said that He believed all races should worship and live in one communion. I knew I believed what the church believed, but I was no longer sure which church. The preaching of my childhood and the practice of my parents was challenged. My faith was their faith; I knew no other. I had come to a crossroad in spiritual growth.

Peter once believed in a faith calling for separate seating arrangements for Jews and Gentiles; I trusted without question the sanctity of Deep South, 1960s segregated Christianity. The Holy Spirit began to redirect my tradition by making me use my head. At college, I had to choose to blindly accept the map of Christian race relations given me by my home church or to believe what I saw in new territory.

By God's grace I surrendered the old map for correction. I chose to let a new map be drawn, ordering the world of my faith with the aid of thoughtful reflection. To do this I had to separate the symbols of my tradition from the meaning of those symbols, the names of things from what was being named. Peter had to take the name of the Christ which his in-group had given him and draw out the meaning of Jesus the Christ. I had to take my church's definition of neighbor and draw out an understanding of my neighbor the black (Hispanic, Russian, female). The new stretch of my Christian journey included a more open stance toward all my brothers and sisters in Christ.

The redirection of faith by a transformed heart does not deny the past, it builds on it. Peter did not get to the confession at Caesarea Philippi without first having been given a view of the Messiah. I would not have questioned who my neighbor was if my church had not instilled in me love for neighbor.

The crossroad leading us beyond tradition does not call us to exchange submission to one tradition for unquestioning loyalty to another. At first in my newfound college church I simply rejected my old community and believed whatever I heard from the new one. In time, I realized that all traditions are partial. My parent tradition was a mixture of faith and falseness. As I grew up I had to sift out the truth, holding to the good and rejecting the bad. That responsibility for personal discernment by the Holy Spirit's guidance did not end when I joined the college church, nor is it ended now.

Loving God with Our Minds

Tradition is not rejected wholesale, but it is put under a new center of authority. I call this new way of discerning spiritual direction "I'll believe it when I see it" faith.[11]

Christians at this stage let go of full dependence on external authority and begin to question the beliefs of their in-group. They chart their course by reason as well as church tradition. They believe what they can see with understanding. What they cannot see meaning in, they do not give uncritical loyalty to.

Martin Luther's answer to the charges against him is a good example of this open-eyed faith. We have left Martin Luther on trial long enough. John Eck had just asked Luther to deny justification by faith alone because it went against current tradition. Luther replied:

> Since then Your Majesty and your lordships desire a simple reply, I will answer without horns and without teeth. Unless I am convicted by Scripture and *plain reason*—I do not accept the authority of popes and councils, for they have contradicted each other—my conscience is captive to the Word of God. I cannot and I will not recant anything, for to go against conscience is neither right nor safe. God help me. Amen.[12]

Luther had been freed of the external authority of his tradition and his destiny was tied to the Word of God as interpreted to his inner conscience by plain reason. The priestly authority of the in-crowd had been replaced by the priestly authority of the believer Luther. Not all of his past would be rejected, but all would be inspected. He had exited the spiritual crisis which called him beyond tradition.

Christian education was helpful to extraordinary Christians like Peter and Luther at this crossroad, and it is valuable for ordinary Christians like you and me. Thoughtful reading can help free us to travel beyond tradition. Peter was challenged as Jesus began to teach (Mark 8:31); Luther came to justification by faith by studying the Bible at Wittenburg; and I was encouraged to think during my crossroad by a campus minister and pastor who helped me ask the right questions.

Higher education is often the scene of this spiritual crossroad. Denominational colleges and seminaries are great places for the crossroad calling beyond tradition to be resolved.[13] I teach in one such college. Unreflective but fiercely loyal Christian students enter believing what the church believes without knowing why. Through study and discussion we professors challenge them to defend their views. This is sometimes painful, but, if they are open, students learn not only to believe but also to know for themselves why they believe. We know that no group or external authority can sustain faith in Christ to full maturity. The one holding the faith must take serious responsibility for his or her own beliefs. We want our students to join ranks with the Samaritan villagers in John 4:42 who told the woman at the well: "It is no longer because of your words that we believe, for we have heard for ourselves, and we know that this is indeed the Savior of the world."

All traditions of faith, including yours and mine, fall short of the full stature of Christ we are called to strive toward. One turning point in this striving is the use of the mind to understand the church we are a part of. This only follows the surrender of a blind and uncritical trust in what the church teaches. Classrooms where stimulating questions are asked by Christian teachers make good greenhouses for this growth. Of course, believers do not have to go to school to begin to think for themselves. Tough tests are as close as the most recent crisis in life, and the Bible is the required text for that course.

Where Are You?

If you feel roadblocked in your Christian journey, perhaps you are being called beyond tradition. Do you find yourself faced with real-life questions but unsatisfied by memorized answers? God may be leading you to ask why you believe what you believe, to find your own place to stand within the congregation of Christians. Realize that no system exists "out there somewhere" which is perfect or worthy of total loyalty. Consider carefully your tradition, but in the final analysis follow the Spirit's inner guidance.

This may lead you to take a stand on some Christian issue apart from where most of your fellow believers are. If you are thus led by Scripture and plain reason, step out, speak up. You need to move on and your church needs your leadership. All in-groups need some question askers and hard thinkers. A professor at our college often inquires of students: "Have you asked any good questions lately?" Have you?

At the same time, remember the dangers. To Christians who believe what the church believes, those who stretch the boundaries of Christian experience and activity are viewed at first as less than true believers. For those who define truth as what most of their Christian friends believe, a minority view in direct conflict with a dearly held majority belief is condemned without question. Remember that Luther's pope and emperor forbid even the discussion of certain issues. Despite this resistance, every generation of Christians faces the task of letting go its once fitting but now outgrown estimate of the kingdom of God. Each generation is called to travel forward into God's future toward a new vision. In your crisis, permit yourself to be given a renewed vision.

Another, greater danger than rejection exists at this crossroad. It is the danger of letting your reason become the final authority in your faith. Those who travel along the "I'll believe it when I see it" path are tempted to think that what they see is all there is. In prayer and faith we must be mindful that our understanding sees only a portion of what our tradition passes on to us. Peter's view of the Christ needed expanding under Jesus' teaching, but Peter's newfound view could never cover all that is our Lord, maker of the worlds within worlds, master of all times and places. I needed to stretch my map of Christian territory to include all races as full-blooded brothers and sisters, but I can never assume that I am now free of every bias. Our eyes may be opened by the torch of Jesus, but we, like the one who saw others as trees walking, await the further touch of Jesus for clearer sight (Mark 8:22–26).

Conclusion

Believers on one side of the crossroad calling us beyond tradition are bound to the beliefs of their in-crowd. They cannot step outside of their group and question the positions taken for granted by its members. They cannot walk in the Spirit without holding on to the faith of someone else. On the other side of this crossroad believers usually still hold most or all of their tradition's views but with new understanding. They have come to see that what one has not frankly questioned one does not truly know. Believers go forward on the journey of faith from this crossroad with their spiritual eyes open, seeing for themselves what formerly they had depended on someone else to see for them.

In the crossroad between these two stages of the faith journey, a crisis arises which bursts the boundaries of tradition. God breaks into life with questions that outside authorities cannot answer. Believers are forced to seek their own way under the guidance of the Spirit. This calls them to surrender dependence on external authority. Like persons taking off blindfolds, believers let go of blind faith and begin to journey without holding someone else's hand as a guide. This is a frightening time. We begin to realize the limits of our tradition's vision, but we become free to go where the inner Spirit leads. We feel the joy of a child who begins to walk unaided. Bible study, prayer, and Christian action take on a new excitement and depth. God speaks through them firsthand.

Jesus was crucified under a sign which read: "The King of the Jews" (Mark 15:26). His death was a sign of the end of a tradition and, at the same time, a sign of the rebirth of that tradition. The life flowing from the rebirth continues to energize the subjects of the King of the Jews today.

Jesus spent His life in the Jewish tradition. He never rejected it, but He did not remain within the bounds of its popular interpretation. Rather, He interpreted His tradition by the Spirit which guided Him from within. As a boy questioning the elders in the Temple and as a young man rejecting popular expectations in the wilderness temptations, Jesus expanded the title, King of the Jews. Neither His family, His religious in-group, nor His disciples understood Him. All rebuked or deserted Him. At the end, in the Garden, Jesus knelt alone asking God the tough questions while the confident disciples slept. At the foot of the cross, the religious authorities of the day mocked Him, calling, "Let the Christ, the King of Israel, come down now from the cross, that we may see and believe" (Mark 15:32). He alone knew the titles were His if He did not save Himself. God honored His rejection of the crowded way, raising Him to reign forever, King of the Jews, King of kings, Lord of lords.

Jesus traveled beyond the tradition of the King of the Jews through surrender, death, and a transformed life. We who take up our cross and follow Him daily will see the same process taking place in our spiritual journeys if we listen at the crossroads for His call and follow Him alone.

Notes

1. Remember that not all Christians will travel this way and confront this crossroad. See the opening discussion in chapter 4.

2. The central characteristics of this stage of the journey are taken from faith stage three, "Synthetic-Conventional Faith," James W. Fowler, *Stages of Faith* (San Francisco: Harper and Row, 1981), pp. 151-173. The transition from Fowler's faith stage three to faith stage four, "Individuative-Reflective Faith" is the background for discussion of the crossroad calling us beyond tradition.

3. See Daniel O. Aleshire, *Faithcare: Ministering to All God's People Through the Ages of Life* (Philadelphia: Westminster Press, 1988).

4. Thomas A. Droege, *Faith Passages and Patterns* (Philadelphia: Fortress Press, 1983), p. 55.

5. Sharon Parks in *The Critical Years: The Young Adult Search for a Faith to Live By* (San Francisco: Harper and Row, 1986), p. 70, traces this maturing process in four forms: cognition, dependence, community, and faith.

6. Quoted in Roland H. Bainton, *Here I Stand* (New York: Mentor Books, 1950), pp. 143-44.

7. Droege, p. 95.

8. Parks, p. 76, calls this inclination to see ourselves according to other people as "the tyranny of the 'they.'"

9. Whether the Apostolic or Jerusalem Council of Acts 15 came before or after the writing of Galatians is unknown. See John William MacGorman, "Galatians," *The Broadman Bible Commentary*, Vol. 11 (Nashville: Broadman Press, 1971), pp. 79-80.

10. Peter's fall from power among the pillars of the Jerusalem church is alluded to in Hans Dieter Betz, *Galatians* (Philadelphia: Fortress Press, 1979), pp. 103-112; see also F. V. Filson, "Peter," *The Interpreter's Dictionary of the Bible*, Vol. 3 (Nashville: Abingdon Press, 1962), p. 754.

11. See Droege, pp. 57-70, where he discusses faith stage four as "As I see it, God is . . ."

12. As quoted in Bainton, p. 144. Italics mine.

13. See Droege, pp. 57-58.

6

Crossroads:
Traveling Beyond Personal
Understanding

The last two chapters took their titles from the feature governing the faith journey just before a crossroad: fairness in one case and tradition in the other. This chapter's title follows that custom. The leading edge of faith at this period is reasoned reflection, with the inner Spirit as final judge. It is understanding, personally proven and held. The ruling quality redirected at this turning point is personal understanding.

The Road Before

The path leading to this crossroad is lit mainly by reason. Believers at this stage are not guided by impersonal law, nor do they blindly follow the in-crowd's compass. They think about the path before them, questioning each step taken to see if it agrees with their understanding of God's guidance. Where they cannot see meaning, they do not go.

On this part of the spiritual journey the main work is to redraw the map of tradition. Maps have keys which explain the symbols used. Believers at this stage take the key from their traditional faith map and apply its symbols to their own road with careful thought. A symbol is something that represents something else. The Lord's Supper, for example, re-presents Christ to Christians. The meaning of this representation changes from tradition to tradition or pilgrim to pilgrim. The believer's faith task is to make the symbol truly personal by finding its real meaning for him or herself.

The symbol of the Lord's Supper will communicate as much to believers at this stage as their understanding can hold. Others at the Supper will never ask its meaning, taking the ritual for granted as an expected part of their tradition. However, those nearing the crossroad calling beyond personal understanding long to know the message of the symbol for their individual lives. They constantly ask: "What does this mean?" For faith to grow they seek to say what the symbol means: for example, the Lord's Supper is a fellowship of believers in His name; or, the Lord's Supper is His spiritual presence entering my life; or, the Lord's Supper is the actual body and blood of Jesus sacrificed for my sins.

For believers at this stage these statements cannot be borrowed from tradition without being tailored to fit. They must be thought through and personally accepted after critical questioning. The traditional meaning becomes a personal one.

Each believer arranges these personal meanings into a map of faith. Their maps are precise and the boundaries carefully drawn. Where there is a tension between possible meanings the believer thinks things out and chooses one or the other as the truth. Trusted outside authorities are still consulted, but the final judgment is reserved for an inner panel of experts—one's own conscience in submission to the Holy Spirit. Plain reason is the glue which holds the meanings together and is therefore a central ingredient of faith at this stage in the spiritual journey.

Let me illustrate this threefold process: seeing the difference between a symbol and its meaning; thinking about and choosing the right meaning; and gluing that meaning into the structure of personal faith. As part of a class exercise I ask my students if they believe in the doctrine of the virgin birth.[1] Most automatically answer yes. Then I ask them what it means. Many have never considered this second question. They presumed it was enough to accept the doctrine as true. The first answer I usually get is that it means Jesus was conceived by Mary without human help. I affirm that answer but then ask them what that means for their Christian faith. After some knitting of the brows I usually am told that it means Jesus is divine. As a church historian I remind them that in the early church the virgin birth was used to point out that Jesus was human, combating a heresy that he only seemed to be real flesh and blood. Again I pose the question: When you confess that Jesus was born of a virgin, what does it mean for *your* faith? I hope that this sets them to the task I described earlier of seeking the meaning of a Christian symbol and applying it to their own personal Christian walk.

This work of making a personal map of faith's territory is necessary on the journey to Christian maturity. Elton Trueblood puts the truth bluntly: "If any religion or any part of religion is not true, we ought to give it up. To maintain the appearance of a faith merely because it is socially useful, or comforting, though believed to be false, is to deny what is asserted."[2] Spirit-guided reason is a right helpful tool for dividing truth from falsehood. Again hear Trueblood: "Revelation must be tested by reason for the simple reason that there are false claims to revelation."[3] Mature belief seeks to map out a firsthand faith free from error. Only then can we say truthfully, "I know whom I have believed, and am persuaded" (2 Tim. 1:12, KJV).

Believers at this point know they have a personal way of looking at the world, their own world view. They are able to make a defense of their faith that is both thoughtful and personal. The horizons of their faith are constantly expanding as they survey and carefully draw out the Christian tradition of which they are a part. Their relationship with God has a stand-alone quality which is unshaken by contradictions within churches or the failures of outside authority figures.

This leg of the journey is not the last lap, however. Two limitations frequently burden the Christian traveler just prior to the crossroad calling us beyond personal understanding. The first is the separation of faith from mystery. The believers we are describing will admit they do not know some things, but they think all things are knowable. They may not know all the answers yet, but given enough time and information they believe they can know all truth. A mystery for them is simply a puzzle they have not solved yet.

In reality, some things about God are unknowable, transcendent, beyond our insight. The crossroad leading to travel beyond personal failure turns pilgrims toward a faith which meets God eye to eye but still sees an unfathomable mystery. To know God is to know a mystery which cannot be reduced to plain statement. The road to God is not always on a flat from horizon to horizon; sometimes we travel beneath rugged, snow-capped mountains inspiring in their beauty but too high for us ever to climb. The wonder and awe of the faith journey may be endangered by forgetting this.

The second limitation is the danger of thinking what one knows about God is all God truly is. In discovering and putting together a personal map of Christian faith, believers sometimes trust the map more than the treasure to which it leads.[4] They are intent to draw closer to the truth by redrawing the standard issue faith map of tradition. If an experience—miraculous healing, perhaps, or a prophetic dream—is not on their map they do not consider it real. They are like travelers driving by a state park, looking at their map but seeing no symbol for state parks. Since they have no way to draw state parks into their map, they assume the state park in their rear view mirror is unreal!

Sometimes we forget to look up and out to the beauty of unexplored territory in the kingdom of God. Before the crossroad calling beyond personal understanding we are like my childhood Sunday afternoon softball crowd. Some days it seemed we would rather argue about the correctness of a call than play ball. A perfect map of a trail or a flawless rule book for a sport is no good substitute for taking the hike or playing the game. Correct knowledge about divine things is no substitute for spiritual communion with God.

The Crossroad

The portion of faith's journey described in the last two chapters is left behind as one enters a crossroad calling beyond personal understanding. Before this crossroad we travel by a map drawn from personally understood meanings. For some travelers life leads to places where this map is not an adequate guide.

Entry

We usually come to this turning point by way of some human limitation. Mature faith lies somewhere on the far side of personal failure. Failure has many levels. Not all failure leads to a crossroad in spiritual growth. The personal failure which creates true spiritual crisis is both deep and wide. It is deep enough to stubbornly and persistently question life's root purpose and our own self-worth. It is wide enough to threaten the glue of meaning holding each part of life together. This glue is the reasons we call upon to prove life under God has meaning. It is formed by patient application of Spirit-led plain reason to life's experience. It is the result of trying to make sense of the life of faith. The crossroad leading beyond personal failure is the turning point where the believer fails to find life making sense but is called to follow Jesus anyway.

Seldom do we reach this crossroad before age thirty-five or forty. Great personal failures may happen any time, but there comes a season when we realize our limited ability to make sense of them or steer around them. A failure which years before might have been ignored because of future possibilities or excused as a mistake to be avoided thereafter may refuse to be set aside so easily later in life.

In the approach to this crossroad, life forces us to become deeply aware of our limits. This is the time when we understand with hearts as well as heads that there may be more years behind us than ahead of us, more questions in the world without than we have answers within. Past actions have closed off certain future possibilities. Responsibilities accepted rule out some former choices. For instance, investing in one career for twenty years means you cannot switch to another without losing twenty years seniority. Putting off children for job or education alters family life later; having children instead of career means starting over when they leave home. There are some dreams we will not see fulfilled, some questions we will never have answered, some endings we will have to face. The groups we are a part of—work, family, church—all shape who we are in ways we cannot completely escape.

Christians are restricted by some limits as to who we can be and what we can do. We are persons with our eyes on the North Star but our feet are in the mud. We glimpse the eternal possibilities, but we cannot fly high enough to put them all into practice. At the crossroad calling us beyond personal understanding we run headfirst into this fact.

We have been busy carefully mapping our way to the heavens. Through personal failure of many types we may come to know that we can redraw the map of faith any number of times, but it will never guide us around cold death. You must be buried in the darkness of the tomb before you can wake to the light of resurrection. You must bear the cross before you can wear the crown. Those entering the crisis calling beyond personal understanding know not only in their heads that the grave awaits, through some personal failure they begin to feel its cool dampness in their bones.

Duration

At the center of this spiritual crisis many persons try to turn back the clock. If their map of life's meaning proves less than satisfactory, they trade it in on another and start over. Persons in mid-life trying to recapture their youth by new jobs or new spouses are not news. Who does not recognize the middle-aged man in the red sports car, his hair blown back displaying the bald head he refuses to see in his mirror at home; or the middle-aged woman dressed in too short a skirt or too low a blouse, revealing more of her fear of the future than the beauty of her past. Some people's faith takes a similar route, wearing the ill-fitting clothes of false optimism to hide from the truth of life's limits. This is one answer to the challenge of the crossroad. Those who choose it determine to live as if there were no limits, denying the reality of our mortal makeup.

Another choice at the crossroad is to give in to despair, to simply throw the old map away and sit down in the road. Suicide is one expression of this refusal to go beyond personal understanding.[5] Another version of this choice to give up the attempt to go on is found in persons who take their eyes off the North Star and start playing in the dirt. They turn away from the effort to breathe the spirit into the clay of this earthly life, choosing rather to immerse themselves in the sensual pleasures of loveless sex or drugs or empty work. Because they find they cannot live among the morning stars they refuse to rejoice with them.

The faithful way out is found in the surrender of self-control and personal certainty. It is a calling to continue the journey of faith even when the map is not yet finished. Instead of paddling faith in the direction we have come to believe is right, we acknowledge our weakness. We learn to wait on the wind and tide, cooperating with forces beyond our control. Instead of only acting when confident of the right way, we surrender to the fact that sometimes we have to walk into territory where our maps are unclear. We learn to trust God beyond what we already know about God.

This is a difficult surrender to explain because it is beyond rational explanation. Explaining what it is not is easier. The surrender is not the surrender of inner authority for a return to the control of outside authorities. The limits of one believer's personal understanding are not improved by replacing them with the limited understanding of the crowd. To drop personal understanding altogether because reason can carry us only so far is to stop short of the distance it can carry us.

The surrender is not the surrender of all questions and doubts. It is to learn to accept the reality that all questions will not be answered. Mature faith can exist without the right answers but not without the right questions. Without the right questions truth blends with superstition, empty ritual repeated in a maze of confusion. Though good questions alone cannot lead us into the paths of righteousness, they do expose certain paths of wickedness.

The last work of reason is to show that there is an untold number of things which are beyond it.[6] The surrender called for at the crossroad leading us beyond personal understanding is to go beyond reason without letting go of hope. "The heart has its reasons, which reason does not know."[7] What hope can there be when personal failure seems to put happy conclusions beyond reach? We cannot say. We can only point to Abraham living in the Promised Land as a foreigner but seeing with the eyes of faith the city whose builder and maker is God. We can only point to Moses, still in the wilderness, looking from the mountaintop at the Promised Land across the Jordan where he would never dwell, walking with God. We can only point to Jesus bound to the cross by cruel nails but bound to God by trust.

Exit

Those who walk in faith beyond this crossroad know more than they can say. The meanings of faith they had shaped so precisely are kept but are no longer seen as final goals. They now use the meaning maps to get them to the border of the territory to be traveled. Symbols like the Lord's Supper become deep and mysterious again. The meanings tied to it remain, but they only serve to lead the believer into a deeper experience. The main question is no longer, "What does it mean?" but "Who does it lead to?" Believers who have not begun to build a personal understanding of faith do not question the meaning of the Lord's Supper. Believers approaching the crisis leading beyond personal understanding would rather read a clear commentary on the meaning of the Supper than take the Supper. Those who have exited this reason allow the commentary to lead them into an experience of the Supper which is deeper than words can ever tell.

On the far side of personal failure, believers are more accepting of their own limits and more patient with themselves, their past, and others. They recognize the powerful mysteries within themselves which are hidden from their own best thought, yet help or hinder them in their journey. They can return to their past tradition and claim it despite its faults. They can be open to strangers, knowing that the line between the sinful and righteous runs not between groups but through the heart of every group, of every person.[8] This lets them see the truth in persons who are unlike themselves. Even Samaritans can be good neighbors (Luke 10:25-37).

Sociologist Larry Platt tells a story of this faith in action.[9] Retired persons were recruited as counselors in a camp for troubled teenagers. Some feared that the older folks would have real trouble relating to this generation's delinquents. The opposite proved to be true. Elderly persons were more successful than any other age group in building helpful relationships with the adolescents. Platt gives two reasons for this. First, the older counselors were more accepting of human frailty, having seen it in others and in themselves. Second, they understood life in terms of the long run, wisely embracing the failures with the successes. This allowed them to be more patient and caring with the struggles of the teenagers.

On the other side of this crossroad, weakness is no longer denied. It is surrendered in service to the Spirit whose power is made perfect in weakness (2 Cor. 12:9). The direction the Spirit may take in transforming human failure for God's purposes does not have to be fully understood to be trusted. This is not to call failure good; it is not to rejoice at suffering. It is the capacity beyond reason to see truth from two angles at once. Jesus' death on the cross was the unhappy ending to humanity's rejection of God; it was the happy beginning of our rejoining God's fellowship. We are sinners; we are saved. The journey continues.

Biblical Models

The time has come to clothe these crossroad concepts with human experience. This is in keeping with the truth learned by those who have gone through the crossroad leading beyond human understanding: a set of ideas drawn from life's experience cannot carry one as deeply into the truth as can life itself.

Another Crossroad in Uz

The tragedies in Job's life led him to a crossroad leading beyond personal understanding. In chapter 4 we looked at Job as he traveled beyond fairness.[10] His rejection of the "fair is fair" path to faith was also a rejection of his community tradition, making him the target of his friends' wrath.[11] The largest part of the Book of Job is taken up by debates with his three friends over the accuracy of their mutual faith map (Job 4—37).

Friend Eliphaz stated the tradition: the just do not suffer (4:7). Friend Bildad supported this view on the grounds that most everybody had believed it for a long time (8:8-10), and friend Zophar spoke as if their way was God's way (ch. 11). Job used his personal understanding to question and redraw this map. He asked only that he not be condemned for believing what did not make sense: "Teach me, and I will be silent; make me understand how I have erred. How forceful are honest words! But what does reproof from you reprove?" (6:24-25). This stand-alone stance demanding only honest understanding is typical of the faith journey just before the crossroad calling us beyond self-understanding. Job traveled that part of the road, comparing his map to the maps of his friends, seeking to redraw it in a way that made sense.

Job failed. No way of looking at his personal tragedy seemed reasonable to him. Job, in his final defense, poetically stated the case of one who has entered the crossroad we are considering. He compared himself to a miner who had spent a lifetime under the earth looking for gems but found nothing (ch. 28). In the midst of his personal failure he discovered understanding to be beyond human reach. He asked: "But where shall wisdom be found? And where is the place of understanding?" (v. 12). God alone knew, and God was not telling. To fear the Lord and to depart from evil, that is understanding (vv. 23-28). Job had feared the Lord, and he had departed from evil; he still did not understand.

Job was faced with the limits of his own understanding, yet he refused to back up. He rejected a return to his earlier desire for rest in death (3:13-14). He rejected the tradition-bound faith of his friends. His words ended with a final statement of his innocence and a challenge for God to meet him, prince to prince, with the reasons for Job's ill treatment: "Here is my signature [sworn statement]! let the Almighty answer me!" (31:35). Then he closed his mouth. There was nothing left to say. Personal understanding had taken him as far as he could go; he waited for God's reply.

God answered Job, but not with a reasoned argument.

Instead of giving answers, God asked more questions. The first one was: Who wants to know? (Job 38:2). What followed had little to do with a discussion of Job's reasonable questions about his own innocent suffering. Job, who had lost everything, covered with boils, was sitting in an ash heap. God's suggestion was, "'Look at the hippopotamus" (40:15, paraphrased).

God invited Job to see the gap between God's view and his own (chs. 38—39). "Where were you," and "Are you able," were the questions raised (38:4,31). Where was Job when the foundations of the earth were laid? Where was Job when God swaddled the raging newborn sea? Did he know the source of winter storms or autumn rain? Could he guide the stars in their flight or direct the lightning? By poetry, not doctrine, Job was invited to see the vast openness of God's viewpoint and the limited nature of his own.

Next God bid Job visit the kingdom of the wild animals, the wilderness places where God ruled over seeming chaos (38:39 to 39:30). Could Job, who sought harmony and meaning in his little world, ever hope to order life within boundaries which must include such a God: the God who hunts with lions, acts as midwife for the mountain goats, soars with the eagle to find blood for her young to suck? Could he make meaning of the God who loves the ostrich, a bird cruel and fearless who leaves her babies to the mercy of the desert, laughing as she runs? How could personal understanding draw this world of tooth and claw into the realm of justice and quiet reasoned argument?

Job's friends resolved this tension by building a fence of traditions to keep out the wildness of God. Job's tragic life raised questions which threatened to open the gate. Tradition could not answer the questions so its protectors attacked the questioner. Job refused to seek security in territory closed to some of life's reality. In the end his questions were unanswered. The world view he sought to construct was swept away by the freewheeling creation of God at work in the universe. But when the storm cleared, Job was not alone. He stood with God, beyond personal understanding.

Job's final answer to God's questions was: "I had heard of thee by the hearing of the ear, but now my eye sees thee; therefore I despise myself and repent in dust and ashes" (42:5-6).[12] Job no longer approached God through the hearing of ideas, now he knew God on sight. Job's old self was gone, he turned to a new path where plain reason could not take him.

We need to remember, however, that Job's new path was reached by way of honest, hard questions. The skeptical Job was the one invited by God on safari through the universe, not Job's careful friends. Communion with God was reached by tough questions rightly spoken, not a loyal defense of divine predictability (42:7-8). When Job's personal understanding could carry him no further, he surrendered to the reality of God's activity in a wide world and was invited to run with the Creator. He went beyond the crossroad of personal understanding.

In the ending to the book, Job's fortunes are restored (vv. 7-17). Why? We do not know, except that God wanted to do so. It makes no more sense than the author of Job, writing to a male-dominated society, naming the three daughters and ignoring seven sons (vv. 13-14). It makes no more sense than Job choosing to give his girls an inheritance along with his boys in a world where only the men owned property (v. 15). These things are odd; they do not fit easily into the scheme of things. The Book of Job calls us to go beyond personal understanding to meet a generous father and the one who taught him how to live.

Crossroad in Jerusalem

Nicodemus was another who questioned God. The Bible provides only three brief glimpses of this believer, but in them we see him traveling beyond personal understanding. His journey was guided by Jesus. Take your Bible and meet him again.

John 3:1-21 is the first scene in which Nicodemus appears. He was a Pharisee and a ruler among the Jews (v. 1). He was also a teacher of some prominence (v. 10).[13] Apparently he had made a career out of seeking meaning in the things of faith. His inquiry caused him to question his Pharisee in-crowd's interpretation of Jesus' ministry. Nicodemus's reason told him the signs Jesus performed were not possible unless God were with Him (v. 2). He sought a fuller knowledge of the meaning of Jesus. He went to Jesus at night seeking an enlightened understanding.

Nicodemus depended upon his reason to take some meaning from Jesus. Jesus' signs were a nut which Nicodemus's reason hoped to crack open and get the meat of meaning from. Nicodemus addressed Jesus as "Rabbi" [teacher], but Jesus refused to give a lecture about signs and their meaning. The tools to finish the job are not in your hands was Jesus' message to the nutcracker. The food Nicodemus sought could only be found if he became dependent upon the Spirit as a baby is dependent upon its mother's breast. Jesus asked Nicodemus to go beyond personal understanding, beyond signs as symbols carefully explained. Jesus told Nicodemus he had to be born again (v. 3). Nicodemus the scholar "supposed by his own intellectual powers, by his ingenious theology, he could attain what in fact he could only receive as a gift, like a child."[14]

Nicodemus was not ready to turn beyond his personal understanding. Being born again made no sense in his system. He sarcastically asked how he was supposed to reenter his mother's womb (v. 4)! Jesus again refused an answer which Nicodemus could get his hands on. As God had done with Job, Jesus called Nicodemus to the unharnessed forces of nature. The motions of the life of the Spirit were like the wind;

they were real and noticeable, but the final source of their coming and going was beyond discovery (v. 8).

Believers could put their sails up, but another power controlled the winds which might or might not fill them. Final certainty about the ways and reasons of God could not be discovered by prying them loose from Jesus. Sometimes one just had to stand and wait for the breezes to blow. Nicodemus's questions had brought him from outer darkness to within the circle of Jesus' light, but Nicodemus could no more bear that light away within his reason than he could carry the wind in his fist. His last words reported from that night were, "'How could this be?'" (v. 9).

Nicodemus next appears in John 7:50-51. The authorities and the Pharisees condemned as accursed those who followed Jesus (vv. 45-49). Nicodemus withheld final judgment, waiting until all the facts were in. He set himself apart from his in-crowd, appealing to reasoned decision: "'Does our law judge a man without first giving him a hearing and learning what he does?'" (v. 51). Like Job, he had traveled beyond tradition, moving away from the uncritical views of his friends.

Nicodemus's friends had no questions because they believed all the questions were already answered. Challenged to think things through, they replied: "Look it up [in the Scripture] and you won't find the Prophet arising from Galilee" (John 7:52).[15] They believed what their tradition believed. The Bible said it (according to their interpretation), they believed it, and that settled it. Nicodemus had come to understand this view was too pat. Without honest questions like those raised by Jesus such a view really meant: we believe it, so the Bible must say it, and that settles it. Nicodemus was trying to solve the puzzle of Jesus' meaning by reason, putting off a final conclusion until he could make sense of things. He had moved through the crossroad calling beyond tradition; Jesus' signs and words were leading Him into the crossroad calling beyond personal understanding.

In his demand for evidence before giving a verdict, Nicodemus was not unlike some of Jesus' disciples. Philip said in John 14:8, "Lord, show us the Father, and we shall be satisfied.'" Thomas, of course, earned his nickname with, "Unless I see in his hands the print of the nails, and place my finger in the mark of the nails, and place my hand in his side, I will not believe" (20:25). Unlike them, something happened to Nicodemus in the dark hours around the cross which let him travel beyond personal understanding. Beyond the crossroad believing was more than seeing.

In the last glimpse of Nicodemus the New Testament affords, he has changed. Language is strained by attempts to tell the change. We see its effects, but like the wind its sources are mysteriously hidden. The scene was set by Joseph of Arimathea gaining permission from Pilate to remove the body of the Lord from the cross (John 19:38). Then Nicodemus made his last appearance: "Nicodemus also, who had at first come to Him by night, came bringing a mixture of myrrh and aloes, "about a hundred pounds' weight" (v. 39). Using the spices to prepare the body according to Jewish custom, Nicodemus and Joseph went to a nearby garden tomb and "laid Jesus there" (see vv. 40-42).

In the face of death's finality, in the midst of a witch-hunt which caused the twelve disciples to leave the scene, Nicodemus served Jesus in the most unreasonable circumstances. No words are heard from Nicodemus this time. The service of his hands was more eloquent than the words of his mouth. The hands of the teacher who once came in darkness now carried in broad daylight riches for the maker of light; those hands eased the body of Christ to earth; those hands wound the linen clothes over mortal wounds in preparation for decent burial; those hands worked with a friend's hands, disappearing into history with the phrase, "they laid Jesus there."

We are invited by these beautiful acts of maturing faith to see beyond easy explanations. The testimony of those actions gave witness to one who was traveling beyond traditional expectations—not like the authorities and Pharisees who could not handle a dead Messiah. They were deeds bearing evidence of one who traveled beyond personal understanding of God's ways—not like the disciples whose inability to make sense of death left them paralyzed. Nicodemus reached out to serve Christ when he did not even know what he was reaching for. Faith beyond words, faith which knows more than it can say, faith which acts when it cannot understand was budding into flower in the dark silence of the tomb. And the hands of Nicodemus laid Jesus there.

I cannot prove it, of course, but I believe that Nicodemus was given what he had been searching for. If he was, his old self was surrendered; he was born again. I hope the preacher was right who wrote of Nicodemus: "When he heard the next day that some of the disciples had seen Jesus alive again, he wept like a newborn baby."[16]

This Crossroad Closer to Home

The turn taken beyond personal understanding is not only found on the roads of persons who lived long ago and far away. The following two examples may help us to get our bearings in a time and place nearer to us than Uz or Jerusalem.

Thomas Kelly

Thomas Kelly (1893-1941) was a Quaker Christian who wrote the best-selling contemporary devotional classic, *A Testament of Devotion*.[17] His friend and biographer, Douglas Steere, described him as possessing for a time "a life which has grasped intuitively the whole nature of things, and has seen and felt and refocused itself to this whole."[18] E. Glenn Hinson included Kelly's writings in a series of Protestant devotional classics because Kelly learned to "live life in another key," because he laid hold on Christianity in a new way. Hinson's students in courses on devotional classics have again and again selected Kelly's writings as their favorite.[19] During the short life of Thomas Kelly a brief season of only three years produced the spiritual fruit and enduring literature which is our inheritance from him. Only in the last three years of his life did his spiritual genius come to full expression.

The turning point for Kelly was a crossroad calling him beyond personal understanding, and it is this crossroad which causes me to introduce him now. His biography by his son quotes a letter showing why Kelly's life may be of aid to us in our travels through this particular crisis: "In your account of your father's life I suggest you think deeply over a question: what is success and when is a man successful? . . . Failure was in truth his success."[20] Kelly's contribution was given him as he journeyed on the far side of human failure beyond personal understanding.

Kelly's search for meaning took the form of a scholar's search for truth. He was a brilliant student who loved the life of the mind.[21] In 1921 he received a Ph.D. from Hartford Theological Seminary, was tapped for Phi Beta Kappa, and after some overseas mission work began teaching at Earlham College in 1925. He was driven to understand the inner truth of things by thinking them through. His closest friend wrote of him at this time:

> He was a bit brash and brusque, I felt, and a bit too confident of the logical and scientific approach to truth. . . . He always desired, . . . to be a great scholar and to be associated with some college or university that lived by the austere and inexorable standards of excellence in truth which he set for himself.[22]

I believe that Kelly was a person Nicodemus would have admired.

Thomas Kelly's burning ambition was to be trained by the top thinkers available. He sought a Ph.D. from Harvard. He took a year's absence from teaching to study there in 1931. He stayed on an extra year for more study and in 1932 began writing his Ph.D. thesis. He finished by 1935 and, though he had not yet obtained his degree, borrowed money to have the thesis published in the summer of 1937. The book was well received by the scholarly world. In the fall of 1937 Kelly went to Harvard to take his final examination as the finishing touch in his search for academic excellence.

The five years prior to this final had been costly in every way for Thomas Kelly. He had been forced to borrow money during the Depression, his time with his wife and young children had been pinched by his writing schedule, and physically he paid a high toll. He suffered a nervous breakdown in 1934 but continued to work. All of these sacrifices were made to assure himself that he had the best possible tools to create a meaningful understanding of life, to certify his reasonableness. All these efforts were undone with one blow.

At forty-four years of age, Kelly world caved in on him. Facing his questioners at the Harvard final in 1937, he suffered a blackout and was unable to finish the exam. Harvard refused him a second chance. For him the failure represented more than a lost degree. It meant that the years of work, the family stress, his broken health, his financial debts were for nothing. Since his youth his religious dedication had placed him on a "quest for perfection and self-sufficiency and scholarship."[23] In the failure at Harvard he came to understand the dead-end nature of his search. He had entered by way of personal failure a crossroad calling beyond personal understanding, a place where his life no longer made sense to him. His wife feared he might commit suicide. His friend Douglas Steere remembers being called to stay with him on the night he returned home.[24]

We do not know exactly what happened within Job after viewing the universe from God's standpoint. We only know Job's response (Job 42:1-6). We cannot penetrate the thoughts of Nicodemus between his first two attempts to solve the Jesus puzzle and his final loving testimonial service. Likewise, no one knows just what went on in the heart of Thomas Kelly during the months of November and December of 1937, but he turned in a new direction. He described it as being "shaken by the experience of the Presence—something that I did not seek, but that sought me."[25]

On this stage of the journey of faith beyond personal understanding his writings glowed with a new fire of intimacy with God. He no longer shared experiences he had read or observed in others; he told of his own life's mysterious meeting with God. His work did not lose its careful thought, but its expression came in images which burst the bounds of scholarship. Kelly returned to old symbols like the blood of Christ, bringing to the return new meanings to all symbols. A colleague wrote that Kelly "shocked some of us still walking in the ways of logic and science and the flesh, by the high areas of being he had penetrated."[26] He had become "a prophet whose tongue had been touched by coals of fire."[27] He no doubt also shocked those who had never left the old symbols or questioned their meanings.

Thomas Kelly, in the three years he lived beyond this crossroad, stressed the believer's calling to let life be guided by the Spirit beyond our usual busy scheming. He urged a Christian life less full of anxious plans to achieve the good life. Surrender to the movements of the Spirit, he believed, would make faith travelers "plaint creatures, less brittle, less obstinately rational."[28] Like Job, like Nicodemus, Thomas Kelly moved beyond personal understanding to a faith that "asks not for greater certainty of God but only for more steadfastness in Him."[29]

Sandra Way

Job and Nicodemus could debate theology and Thomas Kelly was a professor, but you do not have to be a theologian or a professor to travel through the crossroad calling beyond personal understanding.[30] Most of us have been strengthened by the witness of ordinary people who have learned to navigate beyond personal understanding. For me, one of those persons is Sandra Way.

Sandra is a housewife who goes to a Baptist church with about forty or fifty other plain people in Mount Vernon, Georgia. She has been an invited guest in my pastoral care class. I asked her to share with my ministerial students how her faith and her friends helped her survive a death in her family. On Superbowl Sunday, 1986, Sandra's sixteen-year-old daughter Luci, beloved member of our community, was killed in an automobile crash. Sharing with the class, Sandra wept and spoke of friends' hugs, or words helpful and words harmful from well-meaning ministers. She told of prayers that seemed unanswered, and of Christian faith unbroken. She was a living witness to the power of honest Christian faith.

When she was finished, one of the young ministers in the class asked how she had come to understand God's will in these events. Sandra answered that she did not know what to say. She said: "Luci's death was bad and I believe I will never understand why it happened, yet I trust God and know now, more than ever, that God is good." The student tried again to make sense of this. "Why do you believe that? How do you now understand God's will?" he asked. Sandra turned and looked to me for help in explaining what cannot be explained, what is more true than any explanation of it. With regret I admit I tried to explain it anyway, wanting like the student to see it with my personal understanding in order to fully believe it. Neither he nor I was satisfied with my response.

This short scene has something to say about looking for the treasure beyond the treasure map. Sandra does not simply believe whatever her church believes. Like Job, she prayed with friends and struggled with the authoritative directions of her in-crowd. "It's God's will," some said; "It's an unavoidable chance accident," said others; "It's a mystery, but things will be all right," said still others. Aside from the truth or untruth of these statements, Sandra was not helped by any of them. They could not renew her broken heart.

Unable to reach God by traditional answers, Sandra did not get much further by seeking a more personal understanding. Her questions to God seemed to fall back into the silence that Luci's death had left. For months Sandra tried to see how it all made sense, how it could be understood by reflection and conversation, but she could not. Healing came through a dream, in a vision at prayer meeting one night, and in countless moments of tearful, patient pain. In simply living from day to day she began to hope in the midst of a hopeless situation. Now she walks a path of faith she cannot adequately explain. She came to know God through suffering better than she knows *about* God through her understanding. She has glimpsed the treasure beyond the treasure map of faith.

Sandra is not alone. Others in her immediate family and in the wider Christian family have a similar testimony.[31] They have faced devastating personal failure. They have asked the honest, tough questions. They have traveled beyond personal understanding, growing in Christian faith.

They can act responsibly in the midst of uncertainty. One group—those who have not traveled beyond tradition—can act, but they act without true thought. They move by reflex along tradition's tracks. Another group—those beyond tradition who have not yet traveled beyond personal understanding—act reasonably but may be overwhelmed by life's disorder. Tragedy may paralyze their service, reducing their faith to confused thinking that cannot get beneath the surface of pain. But those who have traveled beyond personal understanding know they must make commitments in life while the jury is still out. Life's biggest decisions are made before we know all the facts or all the effects that will follow. Job, Nicodemus, Thomas Kelly, Sandra, and their fellow travelers show us how to act reasonably on "the conviction of things not seen" (Heb. 11:1).

Have you gone as far as you can go in mapping out a reasonable faith? Do you still hesitate to fully surrender to the life of faith? Has your understanding of God met shipwreck on the rocks of grim tragedy: divorce, death, or some unnamed failure? Follow Jesus to the limits of your understanding; then keep following. Jesus' call to follow Him comes before our ability to fully understand Him. The deeper understanding comes in the following. Mature faith is beyond personal understanding, on the far side of personal failure.

Looking Back

Looking back on the path of faith from the far side of the three crossroads we have discussed, we can see faith maturing. This growth deepens the believer's direct and personal relationship with God. Traveling beyond fairness opens up a channel of feeling between the believer and God. No longer is God understood mainly as an impersonal judge but is related to as a trusted friend. Traveling beyond tradition allows the believer to love God with all the mind. Thinking is employed in a consistent and personal way as one begins to seek the will of God. Finally, traveling beyond personal understanding brings the believer to committed action in a bewildering world. Feeling, thought, and action gradually become part of the standard equipment of the pilgrim on the spiritual road. The believer moving toward a more direct and personal relationship with God in feeling, thought, and action is a believer showing signs of being on the right path.[32]

This growth is given as a gift of God. In each case believers come to a point when no further progress is possible without outside help. Something from beyond the believer's personal ability and resources appears and makes further travel possible. God comes and gives the unexpected. Fairness is renewed with friendship; tradition is renewed in thoughtful confrontation; and exhausted reason is renewed by patient faithfulness. The spiritual journey continues, stage by stage, as God supplies the strength.

Our part in each of these crossroads is surrender of an old way. At the heart of each step forward in faith is a choice to surrender familiar territory, trusting God to lead us onward. The next two chapters will explore in detail this surrender as the key element in spiritual growth.

Notes

1. Concepts, events, persons, or things may serve as symbols. See Sharon Parks, *The Critical Years* (San Francisco: Harper and Row, 1986), p. 124. On the difference between symbols and signs or simple ciphers see Avery Dulles, *Models of Revelation* (Garden City, N.Y.: Doubleday, 1983), pp. 131-134.

2. David Elton Trueblood, *Philosophy of Religion* (New York: Harper and Row, 1957), p. 33.

3. Trueblood, p. 32.

4. Thomas A. Droege, *Faith Passages and Patterns* (Philadelphia: Fortress Press, 1983), p. 81, titled this part of Christian growth with the warning, " 'Don't Confuse the Map with the Territory.' "

5. Suicide is a complex act. Not all suicides are cowardly or free choices of rational minds. I do believe that suicide is in some sense a refusal to surrender to God the unavoidable and potentially healing suffering of human experience. See Gerald G. May, *Will and Spirit* (San Francisco: Harper and Row, 1982), pp. 306-307.

6. Blaise Pascal, *Pensées* (1670; rpt. New York: Random House, 1941), p. 93.

7. Ibid., p. 95.

8. James W. Fowler, *Becoming Adult, Becoming Christian* (San Francisco: Harper and Row, 1984), p. 67.

9. Told by Larry A. Platt in a seminar ("Ministering to the Elderly") at

Brewton-Parker College, Mt. Vernon, Georgia, May 16, 1988. For more information on the elderly's place in our society see Larry A. Platt and Roger Branch, *Effective Community Action for an Aging Society* (published under the auspices of Title 1-A, U.S. Office of Education, 1981); and Larry A. Platt and Roger G. Branch, *Resources for Ministry in Death and Dying* (Nashville: Broadman Press, 1988).

10. See chapter 4. The Book of Job artfully illustrates several crossroads in a brief span. Most believers take decades to cross the same territory.

11. See chapter 5.

12. Translation based on the commentary in J. Gerald Janzen, *Job* (Atlanta: John Knox Press, 1985), pp. 254-56.

13. H. C. Kee, "Nicodemus," *The Interpreter's Dictionary of the Bible*, Vol. 3 (Nashville: Abingdon Press, 1962), p. 547, points out that the use of the definite article—*the* teacher—in 3:10 of the Greek text of John's Gospel emphasizes Nicodemus's stature as a teacher.

14. Eduard Schweizer, *The Good News According to Matthew* (Atlanta: John Knox Press, 1975), p. 363.

15. John 7:52 as translated in Raymond E. Brown, *The Gospel According to John I-XII*, (Garden City: Doubleday, 1966), p. 319. Brown, p. 325, argues that the challenge to "look it up" was a reference to looking at the Jewish Scriptures.

16. Frederick Buechner, *Peculiar Treasures: A Biblical Who's Who* (San Francisco: Harper and Row, 1979), p. 123.

17. Thomas R. Kelly, *A Testament of Devotion* with biographical memoir by Douglas V. Steere (San Francisco: Harper and Row, 1941).

18. Ibid., p. 1.

19. E. Glenn Hinson, ed., *The Doubleday Devotional Classics*, Vol. 3 (Garden City: Doubleday and Company, 1978), pp. 167,175,165.

20. Richard M. Kelly, *Thomas Kelly: A Biography* (New York: Harper and Row, 1966), p. 11.

21. This biographical material may be found in Hinson, pp. 165-177.

22. Quoted by Steere in *Testament of Devotion*, p. 6.

23. Richard M. Kelly, p. 91.

24. Ibid.

25. Ibid.

26. Quoted by Steere in *Testament of Devotion*, p. 24.

27. Ibid.

29. Thomas M. Kelly, p. 96.

29. Ibid., p. 56.

30. See James W. Fowler, *Stages in Faith* (San Francisco: Harper and Row, 1981), p. 188.

31. Wayne E. Oates, *Life's Detours* (Nashville: The Upper Room, 1974), describes numerous cases of failure and disappointment through which persons found their weaknesses turned into strengths.

32. See chapter 3 for a description of the characteristics of a transformed spirit.

7

Surrender

Surrender is the beginning of final victory. Letting go is necessary in laying hold of Christian maturity. At the crossroads of Christian growth a new trail cannot be taken until the old one is abandoned. We should not be surprised at this truth. According to Luke, Jesus' last words before gaining resurrection were words of surrender: "Father, into thy hands I commit my spirit!" (Luke 23:46). Early on, Jesus told His first disciples that following Him meant to deny self and take up the cross (Mark 8:34). This has not changed. When Jesus calls us, He calls us to come and die.[1] Every crossroad in Christian growth is a place of death and life. The death of the old self in each spiritual crisis is the beginning of new growth.[2] In this chapter we will look more closely at the key to spiritual growth: self-surrender.

Surrender and Godliness

Let us first review some of the basic necessities for finding our way through a spiritual crisis. At a crossroad in spiritual growth, a renewed heart is needed for finding one's way forward. When we have gone as far as we can go and our strength is spent, God creates a new heart within us directing us toward the goal of spiritual maturity. Our limits are God's opportunity.[3]

This renewal is a gift of grace. Nothing we do can force God to turn our way. Our part is to open our hands to receive what the Spirit may offer. We must surrender our old ways in order to begin the new. Victims of a recent flood saved themselves by holding fast to a tree overturned in a raging torrent, but when the rescue boat arrived they had to release their grip and be pulled in by their saviors. In like manner our spiritual attachments sometimes must change so that we can reach higher ground. Our task is to detach ourselves from whatever might keep us from the love of God.

Surrender is our part. To be genuinely human is to abandon ourselves to the will of God. In a happy turn of divine purpose, the more truly human we become, the more Christlike we are. Surrender makes us more like God.

Our God is the God of loving surrender. God made the world by letting go. God was all in all, needing nothing, but did not hesitate to set creation free to be—light and land, plants and planets, animals and us (Gen. 1:1-27). The creative act of God was not an act of taking things or holding on to things but of releasing them into existence.[4] And when creation needed redeeming, God did not restore us by an act of force or control, but God so loved the world that He surrendered His only Son (John 3:16).

The power of God is love, and love's power is the courage to let go. This is not power according to the world's definition. Anthony Campolo, sociologist and Baptist pastor, often asks his audiences to consider a certain marriage. One partner controls the other by constantly threatening to end the relationship. This ruling partner has power, but this kind of power rules out love. The more an authority insists upon control, the less loving that authority is; the more loving an authority is, the less it will demand to be in power. Love does not insist on its own way, and God is love (1 Cor. 13:4; 1 John 4:8). The nature of divine power is the strength to surrender for love's sake. Surrender is the seed of all new creation. The surrender which is at the heart of being human is also near to the heart of God.

A Model Disciple

A mighty God is pictured in Luke 1:46-55: with a strong arm the proud have been scattered and the mighty put down from their thrones so those of low degree could be exalted, the rich have been sent empty away as the hungry were filled with good things.[5] How did so powerful a God enter our world to do these things? Through the surrender of a model disciple, the peasant girl Mary who said: "Behold, I am the handmaid of the Lord; let it be to me according to your word" (Luke 1:38). In Mary, mother of Jesus, we have a model example of surrender which leads to spiritual growth.

Mary's surrender to God's will was spoken during the Annunciation, the announcement to her of Jesus' birth (vv. 26-38). A poor peasant girl, probably about twelve years of age, Mary lived in the back country village of Nazareth in Galilee. Though engaged to Joseph, she was still a virgin. An angel of God appeared to her, calling her favored. This was startling enough, causing Mary to be troubled and confused, but then the angel told her she would bear a child who would become great among all people. Mary asked a sensible question, considering her humble state and marital status: "How shall this be, since I have no husband?" (v. 34). The angel's answer was the Holy Spirit's power: "for with God nothing will be impossible" (v. 37). It was then that Mary gave the reply which contained the phrase, "let it be" (v. 38).

Another biblical figure gives a sharp contrast to Mary's godly surrender in spiritual crisis. Chapter 3 of Genesis tells of a woman who was not willing to surrender control to God, who overreached herself in an attempt at personal power. Eve wanted to know what God knew, so she ate of the forbidden fruit. Eve's no to self-surrender was countered by Mary's yes. Early Christians noted this relationship. Irenaeus (c.130-c.200) wrote of the acts of Eve and Mary as "virginal disobedience having been balanced in the opposite scale by virginal obedience."[6]

Other Old Testament texts also foreshadow Luke's Annunciation passage. Mary's meeting with the angel has echoes of an earlier divine announcement of another important birth.[7] When Sarah, beyond childbearing years, heard the Lord's message that Isaac would be born to her, she laughed at the thought (Gen. 18:1-15). The divine messenger's response to her, as to Mary, was to point out the possibility of all things under God (v. 14).

At spiritual crossroads we reach the end of our way. No human possibilities remain. Surrender to God at this point is admitting the death of our plans and trusting the impossible and uncertain. No little pain is involved in such a choice and no little hope. New creation comes only through self-sacrifice.

For Mary as for Sarah, God created a new possibility where there was no human possibility. For both women the Spirit led through a seeming dead end to the continuing journey of the people of God. In Sarah's case the miracle was the removal of infertility, but with Mary the miracle was more plainly one of a new creation.[8]

Mary's crucial part in all this was her obedient surrender to the way of God. Her power was the courage to say yes to the impossible.[9] Remember the likely consequences. For her, pregnancy meant disgrace and probable loss of her source of food and shelter (compare Matt. 1:19). What little control she had over her own security was at risk in the call by God to move forward into a new and unknown future. Yet Mary found the courage to say "let it be," and through that surrender the power of God was channeled to turn the world upside down in Jesus' name. Now all who follow the path she took call her blessed (Luke 1:48).

Some have viewed Mary's yes as a worthy example of female submission, and they are partly right. Mary's surrender is a worthy example of human submission, male or female. She is a model disciple for all of us. Jesus in Luke 8:21 claimed His relatives not by blood, but by the hearing and doing of the Word of God. In doing so He affirmed Mary as part of the family of God, for Luke had already shown his readers in chapter 1 that Mary heard and obeyed. Again in Luke 11:27-28 Mary is called blessed twice. A woman in the crowd called Mary blessed because she carried Jesus in her womb and nursed Him at her breasts (v. 27). Jesus corrected the woman, agreeing that Mary was blessed but for a different reason: Mary was blessed because she heard the Word of God and kept it. Both of these passages remind us readers of Mary's yes to the message of the angel, and both ask us if we are, like her, part of the family of God.

Our Relatedness

At spiritual crossroads, we, like Mary, see no good way out. In the midst of spiritual crises, the road of faith appears as a dead-end street. When we hear that a new thing is coming into being we are prone to ask as Mary did: "How can this be?" The answer begins with discernment. By grace from the Holy Spirit we can listen for the messengers from God. Sarah and Mary heard the herald angel's word of hope: With God all things are possible. So can we if we have ears to hear.

Alfred Delp was a priest who died in a Nazi concentration camp. During the last months of his life he was surrounded by the bleakest evidence of human sinfulness. Just before his execution, he wrote of pacing a cell three steps one way and three the other, his hands manacled. His thoughts were on Advent, the season of preparation for Christmas, and "the tidings of our Lord's coming to redeem the world and deliver it."[10] He found himself in those dark hours aware "of the angels of good tidings . . . in the midst of all this trouble . . . sowing the seed of blessing where it will sprout in the middle of the night."[11] He discerned God's messengers:

> Quiet and unseen they enter our shabby rooms and our hearts as they did of old. In the silence of night they pose God's questions and proclaim the wonders of him with whom all things are possible.[12]

This martyr's testimony is a source of hope for every traveler at spiritual crossroads on the Christian journey. The message to Mary is still true for Christians today: With God nothing is impossible.

Our part is the surrender. Like Mary, we in spiritual crises are to have the courage to say yes to the impossible. This itself is a gift of grace, one to be earnestly desired by all faithful pilgrims. In so desiring we accept the sorrow, the loss of old security and certainty, that comes with self-surrender. Mary's surrender brought a sword which pierced her own soul (Luke 2:35).[13] Jesus calls us to die to self that we may live for God. This is the turning point within the turning point at crossroads in spiritual growth. Surrender—in Pascal's words, *"Renonciation, totale et douce"* (renunciation, total and sweet)—is the only way to go with God.[14]

Self-surrender yields new creation. Past surrender of the old way, a new way appears. The dawn of a new day in your spiritual growth awaits a no to self and a yes to God in the dark night of your crisis. Darkness in the world is no reason to keep your eyes shut tight. You cannot pull the sun above the horizon, but you can turn your Spirit-opened eyes toward the place of promise and be ready to move toward the first rosy hue. To those who say yes to God in Jesus Christ the old has passed away, the new creation has come (2 Cor. 5:17).

Jesus' Example

Through Mary's yes came Jesus' divine spiritual maturity; He was His mother's son. Self-surrender led to exaltation for

Jesus on His spiritual journey as it had for Mary on hers. Philippians 2:5-11 makes this truth plain. Though in the form of God, Jesus did not snatch at equality with God, but emptied Himself, becoming a humble and obedient servant even unto death on the cross (vv. 6-7).

The key phrase for us is the Greek *heauton ekenōsen*—"emptied Himself." This is Paul's vivid description of Jesus' complete self-surrender.[15] Jesus poured Himself out in self-denial; in the aftermath He was granted a name above every name (v. 9).[16] Not through grasping but through giving was the power of God seen in Mary the maidservant (Luke 1:38,48) and Jesus the servant (Phil. 2:7). Self-emptying, letting go of a former way of life, is a principle of spiritual growth.[17] No shortcut goes around it. If this was true of chosen believers like Mary, true of our Lord Himself, how true it must be for ordinary Christians like you and me.

Jesus experienced the pain of self-denial. Suffering is a part of spiritual growth. We have already spoken of Mary's anguish. Jesus at Gethsemane wrestled with final surrender in agony (Luke 22:44). In the end He surrendered His will into the will of God. Growth does not come without self-surrender and self-surrender is painful. Only trust in the power of God's love can strengthen us to endure until the end of the road.

On many Communion tables is engraved the phrase, "In remembrance of Me." The bread and the cup served are living reminders of the one whose life was broken, emptied, that new life might arise. Remembrance of Christ's ultimate surrender can help us make the right turn at spiritual crossroads.

The failure of old patterns of behavior makes a space for new possibilities in spiritual crisis. The times when nothing else works are the times when we become open to something entirely new. Be reminded at these difficult times that the inability to see future possibilities is common to the experience of the people of God. We can believe even when we cannot see. Mary's "How shall this be?" (Luke 1:34) is a universal question for growing faith. The angel offered to Mary in answer the sign of Elizabeth's miraculous conception (v. 36). God's message leads us to that sign also, and to Mary's miracle and to Jesus' last supper. We can gain strength from knowing that the crises we face are not unique. The shield of remembrance deflects the arrow of uncertainty. Both are found on the Christian faith journey.

Surrender and Hank's Hand

A closed hand cannot receive the Spirit's gift. At a sawmill in the Alabama of the 1960s I learned the dangerous difference between the clenched fist and the open hand. I worked with Hank. He was a big black man with a barrel chest, white hair, and midnight black skin. His strong right hand taught me the crucial nature of self-surrender.

Hank's life was harsh. He had begun working in the fields as a child, hoeing cotton for twenty-five cents a day. If he left the field to go to the outhouse his pay was docked a nickel. "All day long for twenty-cents a day just 'cause I answered when nature called," he used to say. When I came to know him he was working as a laborer at a sawmill six days a week and spent the seventh repairing and cleaning the machinery. His pay was one dollar an hour.

One day he told me that he had gone to the Lord in prayer because he felt so "backed up." He had a wife and four school-age children. Christmas was approaching and he did not have enough income to take care of daily necessities, much less Yuletide extras. According to Hank, the Spirit had said to ask Boss for a raise. That morning Hank caught the sawmill's white owner on his usual hurried rounds. Hank told Boss how backed up he was and said he just could not live on what he was making. Then he asked for a raise. Boss looked up from his clipboard and said: "Hank, I'm paying you more than you're worth now." Then he turned and walked away. Hank described his response to the answer as feeling like there was boiling water in his stomach.

The next day Boss came to the sawmill work shed and said to Hank: "My wife is sick and this mill ain't done much. I wish I could do more for you, but here's five dollars to buy your children some oranges or something for Christmas." Hank said he felt the water boiling again and had to run to the toilet. In there he pulled from his pocket thirty-two dollars that customers had given him for doing odd jobs. He thought: *All them other white folks give me thirty dollars, and Boss, the one I work for, he doesn't give me but five.*

Hank stepped out of the bathroom and walked over to the green Chevrolet that Boss was cranking up to drive away. Seeing him coming Boss rolled the window down and said: "Hank, don't ask me for nothing else, now. I ain't got it to give." We saw Hank shaking. He leaned over and reached his great black fist into the car on the driver's side. His clenched hand opened up, and a crumpled five-dollar bill dropped into Boss's lap. "Boss," said Hank, "your wife is sick and your business is poor. If this five dollars can help you I want you to have it." He straightened up and continued, "Don't look for me around here no more and don't send for me 'cause I ain't shakin' for you no more after this day."

As the rest of us looked on, Hank turned and walked off. After a few feet he yelled out loud. Asked about it later, he told me that he was so full he had to do something, so he just "busted loose a shout." When he got to his pick-up truck he shouted again. His fellow rider, who had not witnessed the tense drama, asked him what was the matter. Said Hank, "Not a thing. I'm just full of the Holy Ghost." I believe he was right.

A clenched fist cannot receive the Spirit's gift, the new creation of a transformed heart. Whether the fingers are tempted to close on hatred for years of discrimination like Hank's were, or on a good reputation like Mary's were, or on royal privilege like Jesus' were, the hands of faith must remain open to be filled with God's Spirit. Jesus, Mary, Hank—poor laborers all three—knew enough about servanthood to surrender themselves. They gave themselves to the unknown possibilities of a future founded on self-denial. They are not bad company on the spiritual journey.

Are we free enough to go with them? Look at your spiritual hands. What are they gripping when you are in white-knuckled crisis and the Spirit is calling from around the bend? Let it go.

Landmarks of Authentic Surrender

Surrender to the Spirit's leadership is a vital part of the Christian journey, but not every surrender is to God. Some so-called surrenders are really defenses against true self-emptying openness to God. Gerald May has pointed out certain characteristics of authentic spiritual surrender.[18] Knowing what they are will give spiritual travelers landmarks to go by on their pilgrimage.

Aware or Unaware?

The more aware the pilgrim is of what a surrender is all about the more likely the surrender is to be genuine. Genuine spiritual surrender takes place when one is awake, aware, conscious of the consequences and questions. It is not an act of reflex. In spiritual surrender one knows what is happening.

The less awareness the believer has of what is involved in the surrender, the more likely he or she is to give in to something other than the Holy Spirit. In bold contrast to spiritual surrender, Gerald May writes of persons who committed multiple violent crimes.[19] He found their explanations of their actions often contained excuses of dullness, ignorance, or reflex: "I was drunk," or "I was so angry," or "I didn't know what I was doing." These apologies all assume an exception from full awareness. The result was a surrender to evil. True spiritual surrender takes place when distractions are removed and the reality of one's choices is clearly seen. In such an event one is less likely to surrender to selfish or destructive options and more likely to risk surrender of self.

Awareness of the real nature of our position in spiritual crisis is often painful. We become skilled at distracting ourselves from full awareness of our situation. Job's friends were not able to surrender their lives to God's reality. Unlike Job, they were unwilling to face the facts of Job's plight and God's part in it. They denied the possibility that tragedy could come to a life like Job's. In the early Christian church, Docetism was a heresy which held that the sufferings of Christ were not real but faked. Some went so far as to teach that Jesus did not really die on the cross. They were unwilling to surrender to a God who would lead them to a crucifixion. Submission to the crossbearing Christ was not possible for them, for they were not awake to His real call.

Some modern calls to surrender our lives to Jesus also avoid the reality of crossbearing. They call rather to a surrender that will produce boundless good feeling, material wealth, and popularity. The life-styles of many television evangelists proclaim this awareness-dulling gospel. It is not likely to result in genuine, self-emptying, Christian surrender which makes way for Christian maturity. Awareness of the real cost of discipleship is characteristic of genuine spiritual surrender.

Free or Forced?

A sense of free choice is another landmark on the road to spiritual maturity. Genuine spiritual surrender occurs freely and is not forced by outside factors. God persuades us to give ourselves over to the divine will by love, not threat. Fear is the motive behind force; love undergirds free choice. Surrender which is forced is not authentic spiritual surrender. Jesus called many people, but He coerced none.

If persons sense their surrender was forced, it is a sign that they surrendered to something other than the loving God who draws us forward on the journey of faith. Think of another loving personal relationship, that of marriage. If a partner in a marriage senses that he or she entered that covenant through force rather than choice, the giving of self in love has been compromised. A sense of being "out of control" is a sign that one is experiencing something other than true spiritual surrender. The self-sacrifice at crossroads in Christian growth is both aware and free.

Accountable or Not Responsible?

The more one recognizes personal accountability for surrender the more genuine the surrender is likely to be. Surrender by choice in full awareness carries personal responsibility. We can check this sense of personal responsibility for the surrender if we ask ourselves where the blame is placed if things go wrong. True spiritual surrender does not try to shift responsibility to someone else.

Adam's defense in the face of God's questions in Genesis 3:12 was: "The woman whom thou gavest to be with me, she . . ." (Gen. 3:12). A paper I once turned in was graded down because of several typing errors. I complained to a friend that it was not my fault, my wife typed the paper. My friend put the truth plainly. He asked, "Whose name is on the paper?" Whose name is on your spiritual surrender? If things turn out badly will you excuse yourself, saying you acted on someone else's advice? If the signature is not yours, then you have not surrendered. Authentic spiritual surrender is made freely with full awareness and acceptance of responsibility for the action.

Continuing Adventure or Retirement?

A free surrender made with full awareness of the circumstances and a willingness to accept responsibility for the decision is basic to Christian growth at spiritual crossroads;

but it is the beginning of further journey, not the end of the trail. If a surrender brings a sense that you can retire from the journey of faith, it is not a good choice. True Christian surrender strengthens the weak and redirects the lost, but it also brings more adventure, not less. Growth is an ongoing process.

Some believers surrender with awareness, free choice, and acceptance of personal responsibility; but, after the initial commitment, they cease to use their knowledge, judgment, or will. Such surrenders can be demonic. May cites the examples of Nazi war criminals and the followers of cult leader Jim Jones.[20] Both movements contained individuals who made considered, unforced, willing surrenders to the causes represented. But in doing so they gave up personal possession of their own thought, choice, and will. This is clearly represented in the attitude which finds its ultimate defense in the phrase: "I was just following orders." Such a defense assumes that only one choice mattered: the original surrender to authority. This is not the way of the spiritual journey. When all further choice is forsaken by a past surrender, that surrender was not likely a genuine Christian self-emptying.

Marriage again parallels this aspect of spiritual life. At the wedding, a couple surrenders themselves to one another in love. If they think this genuine and deep commitment is the final act of devotion, their marriage is in trouble. The surrender at the ceremony is just the beginning of a lifetime of self-denial for the sake of the new creation, the two become one. They need to stay aware, free from outside forces, and responsible to each other. The wedding is just the beginning.

Surrender to the Spirit on the way of faith does not result in less responsibility but more; it does not decrease the number of tough decisions but increases them. Beginners on the Christian way often are confident they know God's will for their lives. Maturity on the Christian way teaches us how easily we deceive ourselves, how complex and subtle are the temptations which beset us, how sinful we really are.

A story from the Desert Fathers, fourth-century experts in spiritual discernment, illustrates this point.[21] A young disciple once asked an old master: "Why do the demons attack me?" "Do the demons attack you?" responded the surprised old pilgrim, "The demons do not attack us when we follow our self-wills, because then our wills become demons and themselves trouble us to obey them." The young believer thought his troubles with temptation should be ended by his commitment to the Christian path. The old man knew that the young disciple had not yet understood his own inner desires, much less the evil enemies of the principalities and powers (Eph. 6:12). The initial surrender to the Christian way does not end confrontation with tough spiritual obstacles. The way home gets more dangerous, not easier, as we travel onward. Surrender to the gift of grace is called for again and again.

Giving ourselves to God means putting our whole selves in service to God, including our minds, decisions, and actions. Any group or person who tells you that surrender to God means you no longer will have to make hard, responsible choices is not offering you true Christianity.

Some religious leaders have followings built from teaching that levels of authority exist which diminish the believer's responsibility to make personal decisions under God. They teach that if we will surrender to God we will find a place in the system where a parent or a preacher or a spouse will make the important decisions for our personal lives. After the first surrender, all further personal judgment can be suspended. Some even believe that if the one you surrendered your will to asks you to do something evil you should obey because God will honor your submission to authority. After all, you are "just following orders." The Desert Fathers warned against that road to salvation sixteen hundred years ago.[22] We are called to follow the living Lord. He never asked, nor does He ask, His followers to put their brains in their pockets and their personal responsibility in the hands of someone else.

When by aware, free, responsible surrender we receive guidance from the Holy Spirit to move forward in faith we are to carry our wakefulness, choice, and accountability with us. They will be needed at the next crossroad.

Seeking or Prematurely Satisfied?

Spiritual surrender produces a knowledge that there is more to come. Commitments which leave us with a sense that we have finally and completely arrived are out of place on the road of faith. Those surrendered to the Spirit never presume to fully know and understand God. God is always out ahead of us. The divine purpose is more than our new image or understanding of it. We can trust God, we can follow Jesus, but we can never see things from the divine perspective. In this life we are pilgrims on the way, never travellers who have arrived. Because of this revelation of our human frailty at every Christian crossroad, humility in the face of life's challenges is more fitting than pride in what we have accomplished.

Commitment to things which cause us to feel more special or worthy than those around us are suspect. Some misdirected surrenders are made in order to increase the individual's reputation. Surrender to money or fame may be for this reason. We pity persons who surrender their lives completely to getting treasures which moths and rust consume or thieves steal (Matt. 6:19). Just as tragic are lives surrendered to any cause, goal, or object short of God. Even being a Christian is no cause for boasting. Even our surrender to Christ is by His power. "Then what becomes of our boasting? It is excluded" (Rom. 3:27). Self-righteousness is a danger in all religious life. God beyond our grasp is alone worthy of self-sacrifice, of ultimate allegiance. Surrender to this goal does not puff up, it humbles us.

The more self-satisfied and immovable persons are in their understanding of God and the divine way, the less they are like the humble seekers of truth we have met from the Bible. True spiritual surrender is not characterized by the courage to remain unmoved, but by the courage to seek further understanding through self-denial.

Humor and curiosity are two companions of true surrender.[23] The first is a sign that we do not take ourselves too seriously. I am not talking about mean humor which belittles others or plays on bigotry, but the playful humor which can see the lighter side of life's dark moments. Persons who have overly identified their understanding with God's view show little evidence of this humble laughter. They are super serious going about the business of faith. But Abraham laughed, and Sarah laughed, and their son was called Isaac which means "laughter" (Gen. 17:17; 18:12).

The strategy of laughter is to point out unseen connections between things. Jesus employed this tactic with gusto against pompous religionists in His day who could not see where the Spirit was leading.[24] Get an audience of four-year-olds. Then try drawing a camel being pulled through a needle's eye or a guy with a two-by-four in his eye trying to get a bit of dust out of someone else's. The children's laughter can tell us something about Jesus' teaching. Genuine spiritual surrender opens the way to see bits of God's unseen future. Who can help but smile?

If surrender kills curiosity one may as well die along with it. The Latin for "curiosity" is a cousin to the word for *care*. When curiosity is quenched by a misplaced surrender which ends all seeking, then real caring is also drowned with it. Surrender leads us to look farther, to search for more depth in the mystery who is God. Surrender which

seems to bring all the answers, requiring only an automatic
following of commands is the stuff of religious ritual, not
living faith. Surrendered Christians are curious pilgrims
seeking God with joy in their hearts.

Player or Spectator?

True spiritual surrender puts one into the game of life in
all its fullness. Escape and avoidance of life's difficulties do
not make for the pilgrim's progress. We surrender to get into
life, not to step out of it. Suicide may be the ultimate avoidance. It is a kind of distorted surrender—giving ourselves up
rather than giving ourselves over to God.[25] Suicide refuses to
play the game of life at all if it cannot be played according
to the individual's rules. Other misplaced surrenders mimic
suicide's avoidance in lesser ways. People surrender to religious groups who will make their decisions for them, letting
them avoid engagement with life's difficult crossroads. If
you have surrendered to a faith which takes you out of life's
give and take rather than one which leads you more into
life's rich patterns of light and darkness, you should recon-
sider.

Surrender which brings engagement with life produces
Christians who do not see their self-denial as sacrifice. They
count their loss as nothing in comparison to what they have
gained; nothing matters but the new creation (Phil. 3:8;
Gal. 6:15). I worked as a summer missionary for Byron Lutz
in inner-city Buffalo, New York. Rev, as he was called, lived
in an apartment over an old bowling alley. His teenage son
was under constant threat of violence from street gangs and
his preschool daughter regularly got lice from her play-
mates. Lutz and his family lived life with joy in those trying
conditions. Years later I told Rev he was a hero of mine, that
I admired his self-sacrifice and courage. He laughed and
said I was the one who had the hard life, working in
churches where hardly anything ever changed and among
middle-class folks whose needs were hard to bring to light. I

am not arguing for the inner-city missionary's life over against the suburban pastor's, but in Rev's response I saw genuine spiritual surrender. It led him to play happily life's game full tilt. If surrender causes you to feel like a hero, you have not experienced true surrender to the Spirit.

Surrender as Gift

All this writing about examples of spiritual surrender and the signs which go with it may tend to lull us into thinking we can learn what surrender is and thus be more capable of getting grace. Those last two words—getting grace—are the deception in that line of thought. Grace is not gotten; it is given. Even genuine surrender is itself a gift of grace.

In my office I have a shamrock plant by my window. When the sun comes in that window, the vinelike shamrock's leaves open to the light and actually follow it across my office wall. The plant needs light to live, but it cannot make the sun shine. All it can do is open itself to receive the rays. Even the energy to open itself comes from the sun. Our spirits cannot make the light of God's grace shine on our way. All we can do is surrender ourselves, let go and open up to the Spirit. And even that in the final analysis is made possible only by power of the Spirit.

If we are not careful we may come to believe that our opening ourselves to the Spirit is the cause of the Spirit's arrival. The plant could as easily say that unfurling its leaves at dawn causes the sun to rise. We cannot cause faithful surrender, we can only be prepared to be surprised by it.[26] In the next chapter we will explore some traditional means by which Christians at the crossroads have prepared themselves to be surprised by grace.

Notes

1. This, of course, is a paraphrase of Deitrich Bonhoeffer's famous line: "When Christ calls a man, he bids him come and die" from *The Cost of Disciple-*

ship (1937; rpt. in English trans. New York: MacMillan Publishing Co., 1963), p. 99. Excellent reading on the commitment involved in Christian surrender.

2. See the discussion of surrender in chapter 3.

3. A basic tenet of conversion as documented by E. D. Starbuck and incorporated into William James' classic study, *The Varieties of Religious Experience* (1902; rpt. New York: New American Library, 1958), p. 172.

4. See Geddes MacGregor, *He Who Lets Us Be: A Theology of Love* (New York: Seabury Press, 1975).

5. This text is from Mary's poem, the "Magnificat" (named from the first word in the Latin translation).

6. Irenaeus, *Against Heresies*, v.xix.1, in *The Ante-Nicene Fathers*, Vol. 1, Alexander Roberts and James Donaldson, eds. (Grand Rapids: William B. Eerdmans Pub. Co., 1979), p. 547.

7. See Raymond E. Brown, *The Birth of the Messiah* (Garden City, N.Y.: Doubleday and Company, Inc., 1977), p. 298; and David Steinmetz, "Mary Reconsidered," *Christianity Today*, 20 (1975), 4-7. Also, the "Magnificat" is closely related to the prayer of Hannah, mother of Samuel (1 Sam. 2:1-10).

8. See Brown, p. 314, and also Malcom O. Tolbert, "Luke," *The Broadman Bible Commentary*, Vol. 9 (Nashville: Broadman Press, 1970), p. 23.

9. See Luci Shaw, "Yes to Shame and Glory," *Christianity Today*, 30 (1986), 22-24.

10. Alfred Delp, *The Prison Meditations of Father Alfred Delp* (New York: Herder and Herder, 1963), p. 23.

11. Ibid., p. 24.

12. Ibid.

13. Mary suffered the pain of realizing that her maternal attachment to Jesus had to be surrendered to the higher claims of His heavenly Creator. Even she could be His by hearing and obedience only (Luke 8:21; 11:27). See Brown, pp. 462-463, for various interpretations of Luke 2:35.

14. Hidden in the lining of his jacket for ten years Blaise Pascal carried a description of his encounter with God at conversion. It was found after his death by a servant. The line quoted is Pascal's sense of how to take hold of and never be separated from God. See Evelyn Underhill, *Mysticism* (1911; rpt. New York: E. P. Dutton, 1961), p. 190; and Hugh T. Kerr and John M. Mulder, *Conversions* (Grand Rapids: William B. Eerdmans Pub. Co., 1983), pp. 36-41.

15. See Marvin R. Vincent, *A Critical and Exegetical Commentary on the Epistles to the Philippians and to Philemon* (1897; rpt. Edinburgh: T. and T. Clark, 1972), p. 59.

16. See B. H. Throckmorton, Jr., "Emptied," *The Interpreter's Dictionary of the Bible*, Vol. 2 (Nashville: Abingdon Press, 1962), p. 100.

17. See Evelyn Eaton Whitehead and James D. Whitehead, *Christian Life Patterns* (Garden City: Doubleday, 1979), p. 61.

18. Gerald G. May, *Will and Spirit* (San Francisco: Harper and Row, 1982), pp. 299-309; see also Gerald G. May, *Care of Mind/Care of Spirit* (San Francisco: Harper and Row, 1982), p. 83.

19. Ibid., p. 300.

20. Ibid., p. 301.

21. *The Sayings of the Fathers*, x.62, in *Western Asceticism*, ed. and trans. Owen Chadwick (Philadelphia: Westminster Press, 1958), p. 118.

22. Ibid. x.61, pp. 117-118. In this saying an old pilgrim refused to take responsibility for a young monk who desired someone to tell him whether he should obey his bad religious master. After several attempts at getting someone else to decide for him, the young disciple quit on his own. The old man was pleased, saying: "A man who sees his soul being harmed, has no need to ask [for permission to disobey]."

23. See Wayne E. Oates, *The Religious Care of the Psychiatric Patient* (Philadelphia: Westminster Press, 1978), pp. 225-27, 231, for a discussion of the part these play in vital and healthy faith.

24. Elton Trueblood, *The Humor of Christ* (San Francisco: Harper and Row, 1964).

25. May, *Will and Spirit*, pp. 306-307.

26. See May, *Care of Mind/Care of Spirit*, p. 20.

8

Journey Home Through the Unknown

At spiritual crossroads comes the moment to decide against or for a new day. Then, in James Russell Lowell's words: "The choice goes by forever 'Twixt that darkness and that light."[1]

Several images point to the need for readiness in the Christian life: the light rising to scatter the darkness, the knock at the closed door, the unexpected call, the seed planted in fertile ground. Though we cannot light the way at spiritual crossroads, we can be ready to move when the dawn comes. We can be ready to open the door when opportunity knocks. Actors often do not know what parts they may be offered. They must stay in good mental and physical condition so they can respond to whatever call they are offered. Likewise, we do not know the path God may call us to walk. At the crossroad when the moment of decision comes, the time of preparation is past. We must prepare the soil of our spirits beforehand for the seeds God may sow.

The kind of spiritual conditioning which readies us for these crucial moments takes place over the long run. It is regular and disciplined. When a patient with chest pains arrives in the emergency room it may be too late to begin a program of regular exercise and a balanced diet. When you come to a difficult spiritual crossroad, will you profit from a past which includes good spiritual habits and a balanced Christian life?

We will have the advantage of spiritual openness to the Spirit's surprising action if we have followed the advice of

the Great Physician. Jesus said the believer is like a doorkeeper whose master is on a journey (Mark 13:33-37). The
doorkeeper must stay awake and be ever watchful. If the
master's surprise return catches the servants asleep, it will
be too late to prepare the master's meal or warm his room.
The servants must always be ready for the surprising presence of their lord.

Our Lord surprises us with the divine Presence at crossroads in spiritual growth. What follows are time-honored
ways that Christian pilgrims have prepared to be surprised.
They are means by which Christians have avoided being
asleep at the wheel when the road of faith took a sudden
turn. What Jesus says to one He says to all: Watch (Mark
13:37).

Simplicity

Travel light. Drop the unnecessary. At the core of all spiritual growth is self-surrender. Letting go is the heart of spiritual wisdom. Maturity and wisdom are both words we
associate with gray-haired believers. The old are challenged
by time to let go the unimportant baggage of life. Gradually, age calls us to give up all we have: physical activity,
job, friends, life itself. This leads the maturing Christian to
see what matters for the long haul, and persons who know
what counts are wise. Pilgrims at any age on the journey of
faith can profit by sorting out their baggage, discarding
what is unneeded, and traveling on with a lighter, simpler
load. When surprised by the call to a new direction at spiritual crossroads they will be ready on short notice, prepared
by a simplified life.

Christian simplification is like wagon travel across the
American West in the nineteenth century. Easterners
started out with their wagons loaded down with goods they
considered essential. Encounters with blistering deserts or
freezing mountains simplified former needs. The trails
westward were littered with items once thought to be neces-

sities which became luxuries when crisis struck. A barrel of
water replaced a trunk full of curtains; an oak chest was left
behind so the team could cross a steep pass before the winter's snow. The wagons which made it to the promised lands
of California or Oregon were lighter, their cargos simplified. Mature Christians display this same simplification in
spiritual matters. They travel light, prepared for emergencies, unhindered by extra burdens.

Inward Simplicity

This preparation by simplicity occurs both inwardly and
outwardly.[2] Inward simplicity is first. Its basis is the inward
focus on God alone. Sailors who navigated the seas by the
North Star had to focus on that star and not be diverted by
its many companions. Later when the magnetic compass
came into use, the area around the compass had to be kept
free from interference by other metals. Jesus alone is the
risen Morning Star by which we are to make our way. The
heart of the believer is created to point toward God, unwavering in the face of other callings. "God Alone" is the sign
above the doorway to inward Christian simplicity. Keep
faith pure and simple, that is the beginning of spiritual
preparation for being surprised by grace at spiritual crossroads. "Blessed are the pure in heart, for they shall see God"
(Matt. 5:8).

Outward Simplicity

Inward simplicity will be accompanied by outward simplicity in the Christian journey. Outward simplicity shows
in the areas of time and things. The choices we make about
time and property are clear clues to spiritual readiness. On
a visit to Koinonia Partners, a Christian community in
Americus, Georgia, a group of students were told by a wise
Christian that she could look at two of their books and tell if
they were on the Christian journey. Our students assumed
one of the books would be the Bible but disagreed over what

the other might be. The experienced pilgrim surprised them by asking to see their calendars and their checkbooks. Our inward spiritual focus will be reflected in our outward use of time and materials.

The decisions concerning outward simplicity are not always choices between good and bad. Often they are choices between good and better, between things important and things ultimate. I remember a television show which taught this lesson in a way even a child could understand. Two men were in a cave burying treasure when an earthquake struck. One immediately ran outside and was saved; the other died as he paused to try to save the gold they were hiding. The gold stayed golden, the man kept his treasure, but "what will it profit a man, if he gains the whole world and forfeits his life?" (Matt. 16:26).

Time.—On any given day, everyone has an equal amount of time to spend—twenty-four hours. The question for Christian pilgrims preparing for crossroads in spiritual growth is not how to get more time but how to spend time more wisely.[3] This is not so very different from the problem of athletes preparing for the Olympic Games. They must find time to do what must be done to prepare them for their event.

Successful athletes and mature Christians both begin to sort out how to use time by concentrating on one thing, their goal. Inward simplicity of spirit is the foundation for proper use of time. Pilgrims who know where they are going are pilgrims who can judge what uses of time will prepare them for the journey. A popular spiritual encourages believers to keep their eyes on the prize. This is Paul's advice in more than one instance (1 Cor. 9:24; Phil. 3:14). If you are seeking first the ability to run your fastest hundred meters sprint, that goal will order your use of time. If you are seeking first the kingdom of God, your time will be spent accordingly.

Two problems usually interfere with the regular use of

time for the goal of spiritual growth. The first is believing our work determines our value as persons. We are a people who often believe the busier we are the more important we are. We fill our lives with busyness for its own sake. Retirement is dangerous for some people because all of their worth is found in their work. Jesus taught that the kingdom of God belongs to folks who do not judge their value by their workday. He used little children as model citizens (Mark 10:13-16), and how many children think life is centered around punching a religious time clock? The disciples thought Jesus would be too busy to bother with mere children, but Jesus knew what mattered. When we arrive at the border to God's land, we will not be asked how many hours we worked but who we served. Work and busyness can be valuable, they can even be preparation for spiritual growth, but only when put in the service of a higher goal. Put God first; do what matters.

The other obstacle to the right use of time by Christians preparing for spiritual crossroads is using too much time to gain and hold material goods. We have more timesaving devices in the home and workplace than any generation before us. Think of how long it took to cook, wash, plow, or print before the invention of modern appliances and machinery. Yet we are not rested. Personal and family devotional time is probably harder to come by now than ever before. Our timesaving devices do not save time if we spend most of our hours working to pay for them. Few would recommend giving these aids up, but if the time gained by these devices is lost again in the effort to gain more of them, no real space for spiritual conditioning has been made.

Jesus told the parable of three persons who missed a banquet because they had other important business (Luke 14:15-24). One was inspecting a real estate deal; another the purchase of livestock; and the third was newly married. Each of these might be considered a legitimate excuse. The real question is whether their time would have been better spent going to the banquet.

Things.—Time is one major area in which Christian pilgrims must simplify. Another is the area of material goods. At spiritual crossroads, few burdens weigh as heavily on Christian travelers as their worldly goods. Read the words of Jesus in a red-letter edition of the Bible. You will see more red ink used to print words about how people use money than about anything else. Jesus had more to say about economics than any other single subject. He knew how likely our stuff was to keep us from being prepared to pass certain crossroads on the way to eternity. You cannot backpack across rough territory carrying your easy chair.

If our bags were inspected on our faith journeys most of us could be arrested for possession of an immoral substance. We own things that are not only unhelpful, they are damaging to our spiritual health. In a world where fellow travelers die because they lack the basic necessities for life's journey our surplus goods should not stay with us. Where there is more than enough, more than enough is wasted.[4] Excess goods in our lives not only sap our time and energy, they soil our spirits by making us thieves. Augustine was right: The extras of the rich are the necessities of the poor; those who cling to their extras keep the goods of others.[5]

John the Baptist was sent by God to prepare the way of the Lord (Luke 3:4). When the people asked him what they could do to get ready, he answered in terms of material possessions (vv. 10-14). What shall we do to prepare to be surprised by the Spirit? If you have two coats, share with those who have none (v. 12).

This is hard for us. We love our stuff. It is so sweet to us now that we hesitate to let it go in preparation for future spiritual crises. I call this the "jelly-jar principle." My friend Mark backpacked into and out of the Grand Canyon. What he remembers most about the event is a heavy glass jelly-jar that stayed with him throughout. He had refused to leave the almost empty jar at the head of the trail. By the time he was ready to turn and climb out of the Canyon, the sweet jelly was gone, and the jar could not be thrown away. The burden of its weight far outweighed the pleasure given by its original sweet contents.

The Christian journey calls on us to go through our spiritual backpacks regularly, letting go attachments to things which might hold us back if we suddenly entered unexpected crossroads in spiritual growth. The rich young man of Mark 10:17-31 turned sorrowfully away from the tougher territory because of his possessions. If we have already gone through our things, we will not be like him when we seek direction at spiritual crossroads. Travel light.

Spiritual Reading

As we prepare for the crossroads of spiritual growth we can profit from the experience of those who have gone before us. Doing something for the first time is often difficult. From going through a strange cafeteria line to traveling to a foreign country, first-time trips are easier if a veteran guide helps prepare us for the experience. In the journey of faith, a few men and women have lived lives that point clearly to the kind of preparation vital for Christian pilgrimage. The author of Hebrews calls us to remember such leaders, to consider the outcome of their lives, and to imitate their faith (Heb. 13:7).

Though they may have lived long ago and far away, such guides are made available to us in our time and place by the written Word. The place to look for leadership is in the Christian classics. In doing so we are not as likely to get maps which will direct our individual paths as to discover the kind of lives which will prepare us to find our way through unmapped territories.

Scripture

The Bible is *the* foundational Christian classic. No substitute exists on the spiritual journey for actions shaped by Scripture. The Bible should become so much a part of the pilgrim's life that responses to any emergency automatically come from its pages. Notice Jesus' responses at spiritual crossroads. They were shaped by the Scripture in His heart. In Matthew His answers to the wilderness temptations were formed in the words of the Old Testament (Matt. 4:4 from Deut. 8:3; Matt. 4:7 from Deut. 6:16; and Matt. 4:10 from Deut. 6:13); His last words from the cross were from the Psalms (Mark 15:34 from Ps. 22:1; Luke 23:46 from Ps. 31:5).

Choices are based upon some view of the way the world works. These values come from many philosophies, religions, and teachings. Some persons see the road ahead of them as an opportunity for self-fulfillment without regard for what it costs others. They believe that when you climb the ladder of success you cannot help stepping on a few heads. Others view the path of life as a lonely struggle for justice which is full of courage but finally hopeless. Like Ernest Hemingway's heroes in such books as *For Whom the Bell Tolls* or *The Old Man and the Sea,* they may give us glimpses of nobility, but finally their world is dark, tragic. Christians, however, see the road ahead in different terms.[6] The Bible gives a realistic world view with all its pain and failure, but it also presents real people who have Christ in them, the hope of glory (Col. 1:27). If we can begin to see through Scripture-focused eyes, we will be better prepared to surrender to the Spirit at spiritual crossroads.

Devotional Classics

Christians have revealed a faithful view of life's journey in many different settings. The devotional classics are a rich source of witness to these prepared spirits. Devotional clas-

sics are the testimonies of pilgrims who have reflected
Christlike surrender in many different times and places.
They are writings of varied worth, each with its own faults
and strengths, yet all have the common thread of the Spirit's
guidance revealed in a believer's journey. This continuous
thread is woven into many patterns, but it shows through in
each life. That is what makes a classic timeless. Elsewhere
in this book I have drawn from such writings—*Sayings of
the Desert Fathers*, *The Pilgrim's Progress*, the *Pensées*, and
Thomas Kelly's *Testament of Devotion*—to help us understand our own spiritual journeys. Their witness helps to
bring the biblical view closer to our own time and place,
encouraging and shaping us in preparation for spiritual
crossroads.[7]

Reading Tips

One reason the devotional classics are so seldom read is
their foreignness. Many are written by persons who lived in
countries and centuries different from our own. Their cus-
toms and expressions are not ours. We have to sift out the
unfamiliar to find the common core of spiritual truth. This
takes skill and patience. When we take the trouble, finding
our own crossroads reflected from distant centuries and cul-
tures is a hopeful sign of the oneness of the Christian faith.[8]
The following are some tips on how to read for spiritual
readiness in the devotional classics.[9]

First, be patient. Not every classic will fit every reader.
People are different, times change. What is helpful for one
traveler will be boring for another. The devotional classics
show an amazing diversity of type. Keep sampling until you
find the kind of writing which is most helpful for you.

Second, learn the background. Find out who the author
was and what her or his times were like. Discover the circumstances around the writing of the book itself. Read with
your mind at work on the historical structure underneath
the timeless message. Recent editions of devotional classics

usually have straightforward, nontechnical introductions to aid the reader.[10]

Third, read with your heart as well as your head. Be sympathetic to the author. We sometimes read for facts alone, but devotional classics are not newspapers or scientific journals. We do not have to believe everything the fourth-century Desert Fathers believed about the world to be informed by their belief in Christ. We must *feel* what they are writing about as well as know what they are saying.

Perhaps most importantly, readers of devotional classics should go slowly. Read and reread. The depth of understanding we reach in spiritual reading is more important than the number of pages covered. Stay with a text until it sinks into the depths of the heart. As a boy I would take a section of sugar cane and chew on it until I got all the sweetness out. We can do the same with written texts. Break off a brief chunk at a time and chew on it. Early Christians described devotional reading as rumination, which is a word borrowed from biology.[11] Ruminants are animals which chew their cud, getting the full flavor and strength from their food long after the first bite. We can repeat a text within our minds as it unfolds its full flavor in our hearts. The psalmist was called to meditate day and night on God's Word (Ps. 1:2). Timothy was advised to meditate on the nourishing words of faith (1 Tim. 4:6,15). So are we.

Listening Prayer

Listening prayer is a valuable companion to spiritual reading. Much literature is available on prayer and I do not intend to review all or even most of it. Rather, I simply want to emphasize the need for silence and reflection in preparing to be surprised by the Spirit. When crossroads appear, we must distinguish the voice of the True Shepherd from the frauds. How can we do this if we have not learned to recognize the Shepherd's voice by habitual listening?

Prayer is the means of grace by which Christians' personal

relationship with God is deepened. It is communication—conversation—with God. Too often this conversation is too brief and one-sided. Loving communication is more than words. Is the communication between a married couple full if their marriage consists of one ten-minute long-distance call a day? Worse yet, how would the marriage communion be if one of the partners did all of the talking and no listening? Yet many Christians are content with their prayer life if they talk nonstop to God once a day for ten minutes.

Prayer as talk usually accents our requests to God; listening prayer accents God's desire for us. We are to make our requests known to God, but we are also to listen for the divine response.

Could we be afraid that if we stopped talking there would be only silence on the other end of the line? Have we forgotten the power of wordless love? In the silence of a mother feeding her child at her breast there is communication of love far deeper than words. Two lovers walking hand in hand along a beach at sunset do not require running commentary to speak volumes to one another. Turn your attention to God and then be silence. Listen:

> The heavens are telling the glory of God;
> and the firmament proclaims his handiwork.
> Day to day pours forth speech,
> and night to night declares knowledge.
> There is no speech, nor are there words;
> their voice is not heard;
> yet their voice goes out through all the earth,
> and their words to the end of the world (Ps. 19:1-4).

Martha's sister Mary found the good portion. She sat at Jesus' feet and listened (Luke 10:38-42). Our prayers should find their way there also.[12]

Using Imagination

Both spiritual reading and listening prayer ready us for spiritual growth. Both provide images of the world as it really is. The part of our personality which takes images and applies them to our lives in a meaningful way is our imagination. This God-given capacity has been sadly ignored by most contemporary Christians. To be told you are imagining things is an insult in our day, but Christians thrive on imagining the reality of a world not yet visible. Our faith is the conviction of things not yet seen in their completeness (Heb. 11:1).

The Lord's Supper is the plainest sign of this. The sharing of the Lord's Supper is an act of imagination which affirms a past and future spiritual reality, bringing it to bear upon our present lives through the images of Jesus' body and blood. We proclaim the truest reality through the symbolic images of the Supper.

Dreams are the main supplier of divine images in Christian history. For those who know how to interpret them dreams are a ready source of raw material for spiritual imagination. The Holy Spirit can prepare us for spiritual crises by influencing our waking thoughts or by entering our nighttime mental processes, our dreams. Evidence for this fact is found in the Bible from Jacob's ladder to Joseph's warning and beyond (Gen. 28:12 and Matt. 2:19). The Bible is full of dreamers who met God in their nighttime imagery.

If we use only waking opportunities to condition our spirits, we will miss much that is valuable. If only Pilate had taken his wife's dreams more seriously (Matt. 27:19)! We are often like a ship steered according to the sun alone. It makes no progress at night because the crew does not know how to use the stars for guidance. We too often believe only in the glaring light of wordy, wakeful reason, ignoring the dimmer but just as steady light of our dream images. In the religion of some Christians the very existence of a spiritual night sky is unacceptable despite the biblical evidence to the contrary. Dream images for them are useless or even dangerous. This is a false view.

Let me give you a personal example. I am an ordinary Christian with no special gifts of prophecy or discernment, but God has spoken to me through dreams. A few years ago I was struggling to learn how to pray rightly. I read many books and sought much advice. I tried hard to satisfy every detailed requirement for healthy prayer. Nothing worked. I felt more frustrated than serene, more broken than peaceful.

Then I had a dream. In the dream I was back in the little church of my childhood. A worship service was being conducted. Suddenly, with no one near it, the piano at the edge of the podium began to play hymns by itself. We, the congregation, were amazed. The church leaders went over to the piano and began to take it apart to see what was causing the miracle. As they set aside piece after piece, the music stopped. We went back to worship. Suddenly the little electric organ on the other side of the church began to play on its own. The same wrecking crew which had taken apart the piano approached the organ to investigate. I spoke up in the dream and asked them to leave it alone. A sense of peace came over the scene as the organ played on. Fanny Crosby's words which fit the melody were: "Praise the Lord, praise the Lord, Let the earth hear his voice! Praise the Lord, praise the Lord, Let the people rejoice!"

After that my prayers came easier. Through the images of the dream I understood that I was interfering with my own praise of God by taking my prayer life apart piece by piece. I relaxed and listened to the divine music without constantly interrupting it to see where it was coming from.

If you say nothing like this has ever happened to you, that is precisely my point. How many openings to the deeper relationship with the Spirit have we missed because we have not been prepared to exercise our imagination in service to God? Dreams are an excellent starting point, and there are Christian books available to help us begin.[13]

Community Guidance

Mother church plays an important role in the spiritual growth of her children. The gifts of the Spirit are given to those within the church to build up the body of Christ until all reach full maturity in Him (Eph. 4:12-13). Preparation for the journey of faith depends upon the nurture and support of a body of fellow believers. Their shared experience can strengthen the pilgrim to turn in the right direction, or their opposition can limit the believer's growth.

Levels of Support

Churches and denominations tend to nurture certain levels of Christian maturity. Some churches encourage travel by tradition alone.[14] They hold believing what the church believes as the highest value in faith. These churches are usually very conservative. They conserve without question or modification the tradition of which they are a part. The loyalty and personal commitment of the majority of their members hold the institution of the church together. Churches of this kind often see persons who question traditional forms as doubters who are uncertain of personal salvation. Diversity is not well tolerated. Generally these churches do a good job of teaching Christian doctrines to their young people and present an unbroken and uniform front to the world. Persons who disagree with the majority are encouraged to get right or get out.

These churches often emphasize the conversion experience with little attention given to growth in faith. When they do encourage spiritual growth they think of it as an increase in quantity rather than a transformation. After spiritual growth they expect a believer to look just like before, only more so. They can aid persons in understanding whether or not one is on the journey; they are not very helpful in discerning where one is on the journey.

Other church communities allow persons who have traveled beyond tradition to rise to positions of leadership.[15] These communities encourage new insights, study new discoveries, and seek new perspectives on the facts. They usually have a high regard for Christian scholarship and support ministerial and congregational education. Democracy is nurtured so that each person's way of seeing faith's journey can be expressed without threatening unity or the authority of church leadership. Diversity of opinion is considered a strength. Frequently these churches are active in the world and place a secondary emphasis on the more inward aspects of faith. They often use theology or psychology to translate the mysterious into understandable ideas. You can use your imagination in their churches, but you must be able to reasonably explain the practical worth of such practice. Emotion is less valued in these churches and their worship tends to be more formal. They are often as dogmatic about their personal viewpoints as the tradition-bound churches are about their conventional ways.

Within most churches a few believers exit the crossroads beyond both tradition and personal understanding.[16] These pilgrims are usually middle-aged or older. They are driven to seek the treasure of faith beyond the maps offered by either the church's tradition or their own personal ordering of that faith. They are able to return with deep feeling to the symbols of their tradition without losing the ability to see the incompleteness of all traditions. In their churches they are the best hope of reconciliation between pilgrims on different stages of faith's journey. These experienced guides do not blindly follow conventional ways, but they are more interested in doing faith than in thinking or arguing about faith. This doing arises from the hidden depths of the heart transformed by finding hope in the face of our mortal limitations. They, like Nicodemus, can act when common sense would say that action is hopeless.

Our Part

Your preparation for Christian growth depends in part on your believing community's willingness to let you move on in Christian growth. Many church "dropouts" are really "kickouts" who have moved through education or experience to a new part of the spiritual journey, only to be rejected by their former church. A helpful religious community is one which allows the believer to graduate from one stage of growth to another without being thus rejected.[17]

The faith community's ability to ready you for spiritual crises depends upon that community's ability to tolerate or accept conscious conflict.[18] No crossroad in spiritual growth is passed through without conflict. Churches which ignore conflict or accuse the believer in crisis of being less than faithful are stunting Christian growth.[19]

Where does your faith community set its norms for Christian growth? Christian travelers must ask what stage of Christian maturity is expected by their community. We must seek out those who are helpful guides within our tradition and lean on them for guidance. We must learn to live with the skepticism and even abuse of those who do not see faith as a journey in Christian growth.

Substitutes for true Christian community are being promoted in the religious marketplace today. The illusion of spiritual community can be mass produced through the electronic media. The personal give and take of genuine human relationships with all their tensions and comforts is replaced by a packaged product. This "instant" community offers a sense of belonging without the mutual responsibility. Beware of the outward form of Christian community which denies its power (2 Tim. 3:5).

A Biblical Model

Consider the guidance from the fellowship of believers Paul received on his final journey to Jerusalem. At Tyre the

Christians told Paul "Through the Spirit" not to go to Jerusalem (Acts 21:4). At Caesarea, Agabus prophesied Paul's arrest by the Romans, and Paul's fellow Christians begged him not to go on (Acts 21:11-12). Paul nevertheless decided that the Lord's will was for him to go to Jerusalem. The warnings and prophecies proved true upon his arrival. Paul was not unprepared.

This crisis in the life of Paul shows us that spiritual guidance is not found only in uniform agreement. The idea that if you do not go our way you must not be going God's way is foreign to the New Testament view of community guidance. Both the Christians in Tyre and in Caesarea disagreed with Paul's decision to go to Jerusalem, and they both based their decisions on the inspiration of the Holy Spirit. Paul did not take their advice lightly, nor did he claim they were not Spirit-led. His final decision grew out of consideration of their spiritual insights. In the end he went on to Jerusalem, clearer in his understanding of what lay before him. He was strengthened by a community with the confidence to disagree, a community which trusted in the believer's solitary responsibility to discern God's final directive.

The Next Step

Faith is a journey home through the unknown. Pilgrims on the Christian way must be prepared to expect the unexpected from God. Christ appears at our side when we seem most alone at spiritual crossroads. This chapter has explored some of the time-honored biblical means Christians have used to be prepared to be surprised by God. The means of grace touched on here are only a sampling of the many ways believers have prepared the ground of their faith for the seed of the Spirit.

The Christian journey is a journey of hope. It opens the life of the traveler to vistas of joy. These viewpoints are reached on the Christian expedition through courage and love; through going on, not hanging back. The power to keep going arises from the presence of the Risen Christ. After the resurrection, Jesus walked the shores of the Sea of Galilee with Peter. His last words to the disciple were: "'Follow me!'" (John 21:22). This is the next step at every crossroad of faith: follow Jesus, for in following Him the way home is found.

One evening on the moonlit shores of the Sea of Galilee with my friend and fellow teacher Scott Nash, I wondered aloud what Jesus was like in His earthly ministry. Scott quoted Albert Schweitzer in answer:

> He comes to us as One unknown, without a name, as of old, by the lakeside, He came to those men who knew Him not. He speaks to us the same word: "Follow thou me!" and sets us to the tasks which He has to fulfill for our time. He commands. And to those who obey Him, whether they be wise or simple, He will reveal Himself in the toils, the conflicts, the sufferings which they shall pass through in His fellowship, and, as an ineffable mystery, they shall learn in their own experience Who He is.[20]

Schweitzer was a physician, a world-class musician, and a prominent (though not universally beloved) theologian. He followed Jesus beyond these triumphs to invest over fifty years of his life as a missionary-surgeon in equatorial Africa. The Way has not changed; it only asks to be traveled.

In the words of Kit Carson, quoted on a poster in a college counseling office: "The big thing is to do it." The story is told of Clarence Jordan seeking legal help from his lawyer brother.[21] Clarence was the founder of an integrated Christian community, Koinonia Farms, in south Georgia in the 1940s. This kind of pilgrimage was frowned upon in the rural South of that day, and Clarence sought his brother's legal help in the face of persecution. The brother refused, for he had political hopes. He knew what siding with Clarence would cost him. Clarence suggested that his brother go back to the little country church where they had both walked the aisle and clarify what he had told the congregation that morning years before. Tell them, said Clarence, that what you really meant to say was that you *admire* Jesus, not that you want to *follow* Him. Following Jesus, not just admiring Him, will carry us through the crossroads of Christian growth.

The time has come for us to leave the reading and rejoin the travelers. Crossroads await. Godspeed.

Notes

1. From his hymn, "Once to Every Man and Nation."
2. See Richard J. Foster, *Celebration of Discipline* (San Francisco: Harper and Row, 1978), pp. 69-83. See also Foster, *Freedom of Simplicity* (San Francisco: Harper and Row, 1981).
3. See E. Glenn Hinson, *A Serious Call to a Contemplative Life-Style* (Philadelphia: Westminster Press, 1974), pp. 88-92.
4. African proverb quoted in James L. Crenshaw's *Old Testament Wisdom* (Atlanta: John Knox Press, 1981), p. 13.
5. A saying of Augustine quoted in *PeaceWork*, (July-August/September-October, 1988), p. 24.
6. Lewis Joseph Sherrill, *Struggle of the Soul* (New York: Macmillan Publishing Co., Inc., 1951), pp. 14-19, explores the viewpoints of life as a treadmill, saga, and pilgrimage.
7. The availability of copies of the devotional classics has increased in the last few years. I recommend *The Doubleday Devotional Classics*, Vols. 1-3 (Garden City: Doubleday and Company, 1978), edited by E. Glenn Hinson for starters. Paulist Press is producing a sixty-volume series, "The Classics of Western Spirituality," which includes guides for personal study and small group discussion.
8. This paragraph is as true for the Bible as for other devotional classics. The method of reading suggested here is applicable to Scripture.
9. This section is based on E. Glenn Hinson, *Seekers After Mature Faith: A Historical Introduction to the Classics of Christian Devotion* (Waco: Word Books, 1968), pp. 17-22. See also Kathryn Cousins, Ewert Cousins, and Richard J. Payne, *How to Read a Spiritual Book* (New York: Paulist Press, 1981).
10. Some books are published specifically for this purpose. See Hinson, *Seekers After Mature Faith;* also Ian P. McGreal, ed., *Christian Spirituality* (San Francisco: Harper and Row, 1988).
11. Jean Leclercq, *The Love of Learning and the Desire for God* (1957; rpt. New York: Fordham University Press, 1974), p. 90.
12. An excellent introduction to listening prayer is Douglas V. Steere's "On Listening to Another" in Hinson, *The Doubleday Devotional Classics*, Vol. 3,

pp. 201-257; another source which has been helpful to me is Edward E. Thornton, *Being Transformed: An Inner Way of Spiritual Growth* (Philadelphia: Westminster Press, 1984).

13. See Foster, pp. 23-24; also Morton Kelsey, *Dreams: A Way To Listen to God* (New York: Paulist Press, 1978). For a method of exploring biblical imagery appearing in our waking hours see Carolyn Stahl, *Opening to God* (Nashville: The Upper Room, 1977).

14. See chapter 5.

15. See chapter 6.

16. See chapter 6.

17. Wayne E. Oates, *The Religious Care of the Psychiatric Patient* (Philadelphia: Westminster Press, 1978), pp. 231-232.

18. Sharon Parks, *The Critical Years* (San Francisco: Harper and Row, 1986), p. 120.

19. Evelyn Eaton Whitehead and James D. Whitehead, *Christian Life Patterns* (Garden City: Doubleday and Company, 1979), pp. 56-58.

20. Albert Schweitzer, *The Quest of the Historical Jesus*, trans. W. Montgomery (3rd ed.; London:: A. & C. Black, 1954), p. 401.

21. I first heard this story from Ken Sehested whose own following of Jesus has led to the establishment of the nationally renowned journal on hunger, *Seeds*, and to his present position as director of the Baptist Peace Fellowship of North America. For further reading on Koinonia Farms see Dallas Lee, *The Cotton Patch Evidence* (San Francisco: Harper and Row, 1971).